THE WORLD IS YOUR PEARL

My Adventures from Bougainville to Ladakh and Everywhere in Between

GLENDA WISE

First published by Ultimate World Publishing 2020
Copyright © 2020 Glenda Wise

ISBN

Paperback: 978-1-922497-00-0
Ebook: 978-1-922497-01-7

Glenda Wise has asserted her rights under the Copyright, Designs and Patents Act 1988 to be identified as the author of this work. The information in this book is based on the author's experiences and opinions. The publisher specifically disclaims responsibility for any adverse consequences, which may result from use of the information contained herein. Permission to use information has been sought by the author. Any breaches will be rectified in further editions of the book.

All rights reserved. No part of this publication may be reproduced, stored in or introduced into a retrieval system, or transmitted in any form, or by any means (electronic, mechanical, photocopying, recording or otherwise) without the prior written permission of the author. Any person who does any unauthorised act in relation to this publication may be liable to criminal prosecution and civil claims for damages. Enquiries should be made through the publisher.

Cover design: Ultimate World Publishing
Layout and typesetting: Ultimate World Publishing
Editor: Anita Saunders

Ultimate World Publishing
Diamond Creek,
Victoria Australia 3089
www.writeabook.com.au

~ Testimonials ~

Glenda Wise is a real force of nature. A highly creative and skilful artist, she approaches everything she does with enthusiasm, humour and passion. Over the past fourteen years I have had the privilege of sharing cycling and trekking adventures with her, all over our wonderful planet. These have taken us to some of the most magnificent locations on earth.

Glenda is a perfect example of why life was meant to be exciting and fun. She never shies away from a challenge, even when it takes her well out of her comfort zone. Whether it's walking along a narrow snow ledge in Nepal, watching the hippos on the Okavango River, cycling across Europe or hot air ballooning over Cappadocia, Glenda has done it all and always keeps coming back for more.

In so many ways she truly epitomises the motto of 'carpe diem'.

~ **Dennis Dawson** ~

Through her natural turn of phrase and easy-flowing text, I was drawn into Glenda's exciting world of adventure travel. Immersing in her unique experiences, taking in the breathtaking sights, meeting those who shared her journeys, admiring her inner strength, as fears were challenged and uncertainties put aside. Glenda's book is an inspirational read for those of us with an adventurous spirit, who desire to be challenged, and who yearn to leap out of our comfort zones.

The World Is Your Pearl is sheer enticement to take your travel experiences to the next level.

~ **Allison Perry** ~

Glenda Pearl Wise is one of the most determined, adventurous and fun-loving people I have ever met. I have looked forward with great anticipation to this book.

~ **Peter Warren** ~

From rocketing down a cobblestone mountain on a bicycle screaming "I don't know how to get off" to joyfully shrieking on a bouncing suspension bridge in the Himalayas, or traversing a narrow snow-filled ledge with a sheer drop below, Glenda takes to adventure the same way she does to life, with a dazzling smile, and without fail, a fresh coat of 'lippy'. Enjoy the fabulous journey.

~ **Mike Litchfield** ~

What a treat it has been to travel with Glenda on some fabulous trips! We have wonderful memories of her beautiful smile, infectious laughter and many meaningful conversations. We've ridden with her from the time she needed assistance to get the pedals rolling—literally!—to the time we travelled over endless mountains and villages throughout rural China. We've hiked across the Nepalese mountain peaks through blizzards, lightning strikes and the magnificent rhododendron forests. We've done yoga stretches together in the queue waiting for a squat toilet, puffed our way through the icy darkness to see a stunning sunrise, then danced and sang our way back down. We've cried over deleted photos, laughed while playing Yahtzee and Uno, and we've shopped 'til we dropped whenever we could! We would do it all again in a flash. A journey through Glenda's adventures is an inspirational story of the importance of friendship, a sense of humour and pushing the boundaries.

~ **Viv and Linton** ~

There are folk who look at something and say, "I couldn't do that" or "I wish I could do that but I know I'd fail".

And they'd end their days wishing they'd had the courage to give it a go too late! And then there is Glenda.

No doubt the first two sentiments crossed her mind, and all that resulted was a driving motivation to get out there and try. And try she did. And succeed she did. And I don't know how she survived much of it. Mountain passes in outback China, riding across 3000 kilometre deserts in Oz and the rain of Finland on a pushbike. But there she is. A living testimony to a gutsy lady who refuses to let any barrier get in her way of ensuring life is jam-packed with adventure.

Hats off to you, Glenda.

~ **Jon Bate** ~

THE WORLD IS YOUR PEARL

A Memoir of Adventure Travel

This book is dedicated to
The women of my family over the past hundred years
THE PEARL GIRLS

My Grandmother
Pearl Adelaide

My Mother
Pearl Gwendolyn

(I came next)
Glenda Pearl

My Daughter
Emma Pearl

My Granddaughters
Abigail Pearl
and her sister
Willow

~ Contents ~

Testimonials iii

Foreword xi

Introduction xv

Chapter 1: The Jungles of Bougainville ~ 1983 ~ 1

Chapter 2: A Lucky Escape—Bali ~ 2002 ~ 25

Chapter 3: The Human Snow Plough—
Perisher ~ 2005 ~ 31

Chapter 4: From the Cradle to the Lake ~ March 2006 ~ ... 41

Chapter 5: How To Sneak Up On Adventure—
China ~ 2007 ~ 57

Chapter 6: Don't Pat the Yaks—Nepal ~ 2009 ~ 91

Chapter 7: The Ringleader of My Adventures 119

Chapter 8: Doing the Forrest Gump
Across the Nullarbor ~ 2010 ~ 129

Chapter 9: Night Dive With the Giant
Manta Rays—Hawaii ~ 2013 ~ 169

Chapter 10: Rapture of the Shallows:
Scuba Diving The South Pacific ~ 2015 ~ 175

Chapter 11: Rapid Adventure Ladakh ~ July 2015 ~ 189

Chapter 12: Trekking Ladakh—
An Epic Journey ~ 2015 ~ 207

Epilogue 227

Glenda's Tips and Tricks for Adventure Travel 229

About the Author 239

Acknowledgements 241

Foreword

~ Mary Moody ~

One hot spring evening in New Delhi I met Glenda Wise for the first time standing at the reception desk of the swish hotel where we would spend just one night before heading off before dawn on a flight to Ladakh, high in the Indian Himalayas.

I'm not one to judge by first impressions, but I was immediately struck by this colourful, elegant woman with a wide smile and outrageously flamboyant glasses. We were embarking on a yoga trek and most of the group knew each other as members of a yoga class in rural NSW. Glenda had travelled from Melbourne and over dinner that night, she quickly integrated into the group, her laughter and funny travel anecdotes keeping us amused for hours.

As a tour guide my job has many facets including keeping the group together and happy while negotiating with the local guides and support team. My aim is always to ensure that each person has a safe and memorable experience, and I also hope that our journeys will be life changing. Profound.

I quickly realised that Glenda was determined to enrich her experience by capturing every moment with her trusted camera. Wherever we went—into monasteries, to cultural festivals or up winding paths at high altitude—Glenda was always 'off track',

The World is Your Pearl

Outside Mary's house in France

seizing the moment. I found it difficult to keep up with her. Indeed, once she caused me heart failure by wandering cheerfully amongst a herd of wild yaks, snapping away and seemingly oblivious to the dangers surrounding her. We had words.

In a sense, Glenda goes out into the world well prepared in many ways yet with an open heart and mind. There is a certain naivety in the way she embraces the world that is both refreshing and addictive.

Glenda has written about her many and various adventures during the worst of times—the COVID pandemic which has stopped all international tourist travelling and will forever change the way we, as travellers, negotiate the world. Now is a time when we need to rethink every aspect of global tourism. My personal philosophy has always been that the only way to REALLY see the world is on foot,

Foreword

slowly, gently, step by step. Small groups offer huge experiences and hopefully a low environmental impact.

Glenda has shared but a fraction of her traveller's tales. None of us knows what the future holds but I am quite certain that when the world opens up again she'll be out there in the thick of it. She's a brave and resilient woman.

Mary Moody August 2020.

~ Introduction ~

**I stand up, and although the guide I choose
may be no more than a wandering cloud,
I cannot miss my way—William Wordsworth.**

I was born with a wanderlust, and have visited more than 40 countries, twenty of which were concentrated into the latter part of my life in the form of adventure travel. It was not until 2006 at the age of 53, when I joined the Warby Ghostriders group of cyclists, that I discovered the thrill of a more extreme form of seeing the world by cycling and trekking through some of the most remote regions on earth.

My adventure travels became not simply tourism or sightseeing, but a collection of unparalleled experiences. For me it became everything from the sensory discovery of breathtaking natural wonders, to cultural exploration and amazing encounters with incredible people. It not only challenged me, but connected me to people from all corners of the globe.

As a child, aged three, it all began with Walt Disney. He was the catalyst for the direction of my life in two ways, through art and travel.

The World is Your Pearl

My father won the first black-and-white television to arrive in Australia in 1956. He entered a competition run by the Bryant & May Matchstick Company with a challenge to build the best model made entirely of matchsticks. Dad's model won. It was a log cabin with a lady and a man out the front. At the flick of a switch, a light came on inside, music started to play, and the figures began to dance with arms and legs moving as they jiggled up and down on little posts.

When the new TV arrived, there was great excitement up and down Darling Avenue in Upwey, where we lived in the Dandenong Ranges. The first thing to come onto the screen was *Disneyland*. Walt Disney hosted his TV show each week and became my hero. He sparked a wonder of far-off places, as he took us to somewhere new every time. Various films were created around different Disney 'lands'. Adventureland showed *'the wonder-world of nature's own realm'* immersing viewers into places like the remote jungles of Africa, Asia, South America and the South Pacific. Frontierland presented *'tall tales and true from the legendary past'* and took us into the American old west, of pioneers, cowboys, gold rushes and saloons. Another was Tomorrowland, which described *'the promise of things to come'* and depicted themes of the future.

As a small child, I was enraptured in all these 'lands', and one of my huge favourites was the magical kingdom of animation through Fantasyland, *'the happiest kingdom of them all'*. Walt Disney took the viewer into the animators' studios to see the artists at work. The inspiration behind Disney's animated cartoons also had a lifetime impact on me. Hundreds of cartoons were created through thousands of drawings. The first one I saw was the story of *Bambi*, a young fawn. I couldn't believe seeing a drawing move when a droplet of water fell off a leaf onto Bambi's nose. Once again, Disney shot me like an arrow, this time into the world of art, and was the reason I became an artist. His influence went far and wide.

~ Introduction ~

When I was six, two documentaries were shown at our school. A film projector was set up behind rows of wooden pews in the foyer outside our headmaster's office. The first film projected onto the wall was about a tribe of Pygmies living deep inside the jungles of Africa. The second was of an arctic explorer, Harold Thornton, the father of Anne, one of the children in my class.

I was dazzled by visions of jungles with tropical vegetation and the lives of a race of tiny people living and surviving on their own with no shops to buy their food. Never having seen snow or ice before, I was also in awe of Mr Thornton and his friends picking their way through it. Getting a glimpse of both these far-off places was utterly amazing to me. I think this must have been the first spark of a desire to explore. I longed to experience the world and its wonders.

Fascinated by the ways of life of so many cultures, I continued to research books, such as our neighbour's encyclopedia, and to watch any film about the outside world.

I grew up in a very controlled household, and had neither the freedom nor the means to think of travel. There was no question of going off to experience life for myself. Apart from family caravanning holidays, travel for me was non-existent until my mid-twenties. I started to pore over travel brochures after I met my future husband, Peter.

A long time before we were married, we took a short tour of Malaysia in 1972, then saved up to travel again, this time on an organised bus tour to see the tourist attractions throughout the main countries of Europe in 1976. Over a period of six weeks, we saw all the major highlights, visiting opulent palaces, cathedrals and castles, and colourful festivals, fairs and marketplaces. It was remarkable to me that, for such a relatively small continent, the concentration of religious and wartime history, and variations of ancient architectures were so vast.

The World is Your Pearl

In Holland, I loved the windmills, tulip farms and canals. Along the Rhine Valley, we ate and drank in beer halls in small German villages. Travelling up into the Alps of Austria and Switzerland, we were dazzled by a wonderland of snow-capped alpine peaks, contrasted with lush green pastures. We ate pasta and drank red wine overlooking the azure sea of the Mediterranean coast. We visited Italy, with its rich cities of Rome, Florence and Venice; Paris, with its glorious palaces and cathedrals; French chateaux throughout the Bordeaux region; and the flamenco dancers and fishing villages in Spain. Each country had its own flavour and extreme beauty.

We travelled back to London from Paris on a ferry, and hired a car to explore England, Scotland and Wales. Staying in farmhouses and manor houses, we lived with the local people for a further three weeks.

Our epic holiday finished with a stay in Greece and a five-day cruise of the Mediterranean islands of Mykonos, Rhodes, Crete, Piraeus and Santorini.

This was a huge whirlwind trip and a convenient way to see the essence of a lot of places in a short time. The only pitfall was that the group dynamics of the large busload of elderly tourists we travelled with throughout Europe were of the retired set, and it was a long time for us to be stuck together.

Peter and I were married two years later in 1978 and knuckled down to buy a house, with no further thought of any spending on travel.

Five years later, my first taste of adventure was provided by my brother, who lived and worked in Bougainville. He knew I'd love the jungles and the lifestyles of its people and invited me over, paying my airfares, to experience the wild and remote places of Papua New Guinea, which was, and still remains, one of the best times of my life.

~ Introduction ~

Our children came along in 1984 and 1985. The joy of motherhood exceeded my wildest dreams, and the next nineteen years were devoted to my son, Cameron, and daughter, Emma.

In 2000, Peter and I parted company while still remaining friends. He moved out and ensured I wasn't left with the burden of a mortgage. Cameron worked for a construction company and also moved out some months later.

I was teaching art, and Emma had a part-time job in a bakery. We were both able to save some money. In 2002, we purchased large backpacks and travelled through Italy for a month, staying in YMCA and backpacker accommodations. Emma was seventeen. This was a unique experience for both of us as we gypsied all over Italy by means of public transport, though we did it hard. Travelling without an itinerary or the help of Google meant that we made a few mistakes along the way and spent a lot of time waiting for buses and trains.

Because we'd done the trip on such a shoestring, we came home with enough money to go to Bali the same year.

Our backpacks were hauled out again four years later in 2006 to trek the Overland Track in Tasmania from Cradle Mountain to Lake St Clair. This was a spectacular undertaking for both of us, and a feat of endurance for me to carry 20 kilograms for 100 kilometres. Emma was fit and young and able-bodied.

It was in this year that my long-awaited yen for world adventure unexpectedly fell into place with the plan of a cycling trip to China in 2007. This was immediately followed by a further cycling trip to another region of China in 2008, and a trek through Nepal in 2009. I became hooked. I could not stop, as the adventures continued to the present day. The trick was to book each trip a year ahead, pay the deposit, then pay it off ahead of time.

The World is Your Pearl

In 2012, Cameron, Emma and I attended respective two-day dive courses and attained our PADI, Level 2 International Scuba Diving licences. These came in useful on our trip the following year to Hawaii where we went reef and wreck diving off the coast of Oahu, and on a night dive with the manta rays off the big island of Hawaii (although this *dive* for me is described differently within these pages).

Anyone with a medium level of fitness can experience adventure. All it takes is a desire to go for it, to choose where to go, some sensible preparation and, for a reasonable amount of money; the World Expeditions experts do the rest with teams of hundreds of support people behind the scenes worldwide. Their experts research the areas, terrain, conditions and accommodations (many times in the homes of the tribes or cultures to be visited). They book the flights and transfers, and provide quality bikes and camping equipment, energy-sustaining food and clean drinking water. Also employed are the cooks, guides, Sherpas, porters, mules, yaks and pack horses. To do this alone would cost a fortune, and wouldn't be half the fun as travelling with like-minded people.

For me to leave home and be immersed into another culture can have a varying effect from total relaxation to pure adrenaline. The small groups I travel with are brought together with lifelong memories and the most amazing stories to tell, as we visit areas off the beaten track. It is both exciting and exhilarating. Being able to experience the ancient customs and lifestyles of many cultures, I have learned about their traditional lives at a deep level in a sustainable way. It is a huge privilege to witness these ways of life before progress changes them forever.

Apart from actually getting there, this mindful way of exploring by human power on foot or by bicycle is gentle on the earth, and with experienced guidance, all the worry is taken out of it. These

~ Introduction ~

encounters have become some of the greatest highlights of my existence. The small groups of people who join these World Expeditions are from all walks of life, and we become bonded forever through our experiences. *The World Is Your Pearl* is only a snippet from the many travel journals I've kept.

I have listed many of my trips below, though this story describes just a few of the *experiences* which I discovered can only be had through a different form of travel, and for me, is the only way to go.

My *adventure* travels are shown in bold, and those conducted by World Expeditions are tagged with an asterisk.

1972: Malaysia, Singapore, Malacca, Kuala Lumpur, Penang
1976: England, Scotland, Wales, Holland, France, Germany, Belgium, Switzerland, Italy, Spain, Greece, Mediterranean Islands, Crete, Mykonos, Rhodes, Santorini, Piraeus
1983: Bougainville, Papua New Guinea
2002: Italy (Backpacking)
2002: Bali
2003: Bali
2004: Bali
2005: Perisher (skiing)
2006: Adelaide
2006: Tasmanian Overland Track (Backpacking/Trekking)
2006: Karratha
2007: China, Tiger Leaping Gorge (Ghostriders—Cycling)
2008: China, Karst Mountains, Guiyang to Yangshuo (Ghostriders—Cycling)
2009: *Nepal, Kathmandu, Annapurna, Pokerah (Ghostriders—Trekking)
2009: Thailand
2010: Nullarbor (Cycling)
2011: Italy, Rome, Bologna, France, Ukraine

The World is Your Pearl

2011:	**Vietnam,** Hanoi to Ho Chi Minh (Cycling)
2012:	***Africa,** Botswana, Zimbabwe, Kalahari Desert, Namibia (Ghostriders)
2012:	***Turkey, *Greece,** Santorini (Ghostriders—Cycling/Trekking)
2013:	Tasmania
2013:	**Hawaii** (Scuba Diving)
2013:	***France,** Paris to Le Croisic—West Atlantic Coast (Ghostriders)
2013:	Los Angeles, Disneyland, New York
2014:	Singapore
2014:	Vietnam
2014:	***Finland, *Sweden, *Russia, *Latvia, *Estonia** (Ghostriders)
2015:	**South Pacific,** Noumea, New Caledonia, Vila Vanuatu (Scuba Diving)
2015:	***India, Delhi,** *Kashmir (Mary Moody)
2015:	***Leh, Ladakh** (Mary Moody: Yoga—Trekking)
2015:	*Srinagar, Agra, Rajasthan
2016:	Broome, Darwin
2017:	***Morocco,** Marrakesh, High Atlas Mountains (Mary Moody Trekking)
2017:	*France (Mary Moody)
2017:	*Dubai
2017:	Cairns
2018:	***South America, *Peru, *Argentina, *Brazil** (Ghostriders)
2019:	***Mongolia** (Mary Moody—Trekking)
2019:	*Japan
2019:	Tasmania
2020:	Bali
2010:	Mexico, ***Cuba** (Ghostriders—Cycling)

There are many places I'd still love to see: Bhutan; the Amazon Jungle; an island hop through the Mediterranean Sea on a yacht; exploring Iceland; remote forests of Japan; Portugal; Pakistan; Ireland; Poland; coastal islands off Croatia; Slovenia; Serbia; Albania; Sarajevo; Armenia; scuba diving through the Caribbean and other pristine waters around the world.

~ Introduction ~

My greatest love is of tropical islands, and I would love to find a coral reef with the colour and sea life I had once seen off Sohano Island in the Buka passage in Bougainville.

Meanwhile, join me on a handful of my adventures.

CHAPTER 1

The Jungles of Bougainville ~ 1983 ~

Once the travel bug bites there is no known antidote, and I know that I shall be happily infected until the end of my days—Michael Palin.

My yen for adventure began with my brother Steve. When he was 18 and I was 21, the family moved to the Isle of Sorrento on Queensland's Gold Coast where Dad built a beautiful home on a canal. Steve and I worked for the mining company, Mineral Deposits Limited. I was in administration, and Steve was apprenticed as a welder and attained specialised welding certificates.

Some years later, when I was living in Melbourne with Peter, a former colleague came in and told Steve he was working in gold and copper mines in Bougainville, Papua New Guinea, and making a fortune. Steve gave his notice and enlisted for work in Bougainville too. He was 24 years old.

The World is Your Pearl

Steve and I were close. He wrote me a letter describing the tropical paradise where he lived and worked, saying, "You've gotta get over here" and enclosed a flight ticket.

At that time, if a woman wished to travel overseas, she was required to have written permission from her husband and her employer. I had worked for nine years as secretary to Mike Buxton, Director of Myer Stores, Australia. Both he and Peter had a bit of fun playing cat and mouse as they respectively made me squirm, suggesting it wouldn't be pertinent to allow me permission, as a woman such as myself could well find herself in a 'sticky situation' in the wilds of Papua New Guinea.

However, after a lot of banter and with their blessings, on Saturday, January 8, 1983, I left for Port Moresby. On the flight I met a man called George with a dear little Papuan child called Diane, beaming with her baby-tooth smile and fuzzy hair in a topknot, all dressed in lemon. I was not sure of their connection; however, George was very helpful. His destination was Port Moresby, but when we landed, he went out of his way to see me safely onto the plane to Kieta, Bougainville. If he hadn't been there I would surely have missed the flight. I had no idea about procedures and I was told the PNG nationals were often not very helpful. The Port Moresby Airport was pretty overwhelming compared to the few airports I'd seen. It was just a large shed with a concrete floor, and not much to it. I felt very conspicuous as though being watched by a thousand eyes. There was a very strong smell of ammonia, and what appeared to be splotches of blood everywhere all over the floor.

This, I discovered, was betel-nut spittle. The seed of the fruit of the Areca palm was chewed by various cultural groups and individuals, and used as a stimulant drug, which was unfortunately carcinogenic. It gave a sense of euphoria and well-being. The user's mouth, teeth and gums were discoloured a dark red-brown colour, and stimulated the flow of saliva, causing the chewer to spit.

The Jungles of Bougainville ~ 1983 ~

It was hot and steamy. Indigenous men, women and children were lying around everywhere on the airport floor, chewing their betel-nuts and staring. I suppose I did stand out as a 29-year-old Aussie woman with blonde hair and lipstick.

There was not much assistance to be found, as there were no flight desks as I knew them. Fortunately George made all the arrangements for me, running all over the airport, as things had altered since he'd been there a month prior. I waited by his trolley of luggage with little Diane sitting on the cases. I was very glad of George's help, and eventually walked through the gates and hopped on the 'Betel-nut Express'.

Bougainville is an island of Papua New Guinea. It is located in the northern Solomon Islands archipelago of the Melanesia region, in the South Pacific Ocean.

I landed on the Kieta airstrip after twelve hours of weary travelling since leaving home, to see Steve and his friend Elizabeth waiting to greet me. Liz was smiling and friendly, and made me very welcome. She was from Buka Island in the north of Bougainville, and worked as a scientific analyst in the Environmental and Chemical Testing Laboratory for BCL (Bougainville Copper Limited). They were waiting inside the little tin shed which was Kieta Airport, and were such a welcome sight.

Steve was very glad to see me and said so, so many times it made it all worthwhile. I wondered how I would go with him as he'd changed his lifestyle so much since leaving Australia. His life was very remote on an island with far less rules and regulations than back in Australia, and there was a distinct element of danger all around, both at the mine site and in the jungles. However, he was in his element and nothing fazed him.

Steve, Elizabeth and I walked to his shining white Hilux 4WD Ute. It was his pride and joy. From an Esky in the back he pulled out

The World is Your Pearl

three wine glasses and three small bottles of wine to toast my arrival while we waited for my case to come through. It eventually arrived with the handle broken and wired up.

Steve gave me the keys and said his Ute was mine to drive whenever I wanted while I was there, and told me it was okay to drink and drive as there were no laws against it. So we drove along with our drinks, as 'Rocky III' played on the sound system.

Steve did, however, need to outline a few rules:

1) Don't go any further south than the airport without him, as the nationals down there weren't too hospitable.
2) Don't stand under a coconut tree as a hit on the head from a falling coconut will kill you!
3) Never open the door or go outside on your own after dark.

When I'd landed, we came in on an airstrip which ran parallel with the Pacific Ocean. The waves were crashing in on one side of the plane, while coconut palms swayed on the other. Now in Steve's Ute, we travelled along a road through an intensely beautiful paradise of dense tropical jungle and magnificent white sandy beaches. It was a natural wilderness where nothing was contrived. Small sac-sacs, which were huts made of sago palm leaves, were dotted along the sides of the road. Nationals wandered along in brightly coloured lap-laps, shorts or trousers, chewing their betel-nuts or drinking San Miguel beer. Everyone was so relaxed.

We stopped at a motel called the Davara where we had a quiet drink and chatted together about the future. We talked to an old man from Rabaul who had lived on Bougainville Island for fourteen years. His name was Fuji. He spoke of the war years and the invasion of the Japanese onto the island, the bombings and air raids. He spoke in pidgin, a blend of Melanesian and English, but I understood everything he said. He was the motel's

The Jungles of Bougainville ~ 1983 ~

chef and said to come back on Friday as he was cooking Chinese food. We'd missed out, because last week he'd cooked up mud crabs and lobsters.

We left and went to the leave-house in Arawa where the three of us were to stay. The term leave-house is a form of house-sit while the permanent residents were away on leave.

The house was high set, with four bedrooms and fitted out inside with every convenience. There were double-deadlocked windows and doors, sealed off with wooden and iron bars. Fans and air conditioners ran day and night in every room.

We locked my case inside then went out again to visit Terry, an electrician in Section Five. He had been asleep for half an hour after a full work shift when we arrived. No problem; he showered and shaved and sat down to make plans for the evening's entertainment at the Coastal Club.

Dotted along the road to Panguna were painted skull and crossbones to mark where so many people had been killed in cars from going over the cliff while speeding and drink driving around the bends. This place was wild, where everyone worked hard and played hard, and they drank, a lot.

It was an extreme life in so many ways. The weather was hot and steamy. Every day at midday the rain came down in a wall of water. This humidity meant everything was damp *all the time*. Cuts and scratches never healed. One of Steve's mates got a fish hook caught in his leg and it became a terrible ulcerated mess. He had to fly back to Australia to have it treated.

Next stop was Steve's room in the mine complex at Panguna. It was very small. A bed, a table, a cupboard and two plants. Hanging on the wall were some arrows and a hand-carved comb which

The World is Your Pearl

his houseboy had given him. A coconut hung from the ceiling in a macramé sling.

The shared bathroom arrangements were down the hall. I am constantly blessed with good fortune, as the timing of the visit to see Steve's accommodations coincided with a sudden onset of a severe upset stomach, possibly caused by the change of water. A few people had arrived in Steve's room to be introduced to me. I whispered to Steve that I urgently had to get to the bathroom. When I returned, I turned scarlet with humiliation when one of the guys greeted me loudly, saying, "Have ya got a dose of the shits, love?" I did feel violently ill, and must have looked really washed out. The guy said, "Come with me." He took me out through the compound to the mess hall, and arranged for a bowl of plain cooked rice and a banana. He mashed the banana and mixed it into the rice. Handing it to me with a spoon, he said, "Here, eat this. Works every time." And it did. I began to feel much better quite quickly.

From there we went to the Coastal Club to meet the crew and have another drink. *Watership Down* played on the screen. This animated movie seemed too cute to be entertainment for a big group of burly, beer-swilling mining men.

I was terribly tired by this time and was so bushed I could hardly stand up. By the time we left, my head was ready to split with a terrific headache. Steve introduced me around to dozens of people, all fun, easy to talk to, natural and easygoing. We talked all the way back and I was very glad to find my bed when we got home.

It felt extremely hot due to the humidity, though it was only 32 degrees Celsius. I went to bed but couldn't sleep. I lay there worrying about things. Steve had told me he'd been attacked a little over a week ago. He had a huge scar across his scull where a national had smashed a chair over his head on New Year's Eve. He'd spent the night in hospital and had the stitches out the

The Jungles of Bougainville ~ 1983 ~

following week, just before I arrived. The attacker had come at Steve from behind for no apparent reason and a brawl broke out. It was on for young and old. Seventy people fighting with bottles flying everywhere.

This gave me the 'dingbats', a term our father used to describe feelings of unease whenever I had a nightmare as a child. He'd come in and say, "Have you got the dingbats, sweetheart?"

Steve went on to emphasise the 'must nots' very strongly. I had to realise I was visiting a place where the indigenous customs and methods of dealing with things were completely different to anything I was used to.

4) If you're out driving with Liz and you hit a national on the road, keep going. If you stop to help, they'll come from nowhere and kill you—no questions asked. They're not interested in explanations about the fact that it was an accident or how it happened—you're dead! Payback killings are how they deal with things over here. The police can't help.

5) The same goes if you hit a pig. Pigs are their most prized possessions of great status and wealth. Therefore if you hit one, the nationals will be after you and if they don't kill or maim you, the cost to you in kina for compensation will be exorbitant.

I woke at 4:00 a.m. to the sound of someone getting up, and couldn't get back to sleep. The worries started again. I lay there thinking about the fact that I couldn't drink the water. What would happen if I got sick? Would there be expat doctors or national doctors in the hospitals? Steve had said, "You don't get sick on Bougainville—the hospitals aren't worth knowing about." What would I do with myself for two weeks? etc. ... zzz

The World is Your Pearl

At last, morning came. At 6:00 a.m. Steve was banging and crashing through the kitchen as he always had. His normal start to the day.

My head still ached as I got up and went to join them for breakfast. I tried to explain my fears and the 'dingbats' of the night before but it seemed very melodramatic, and I couldn't describe the terrible apprehensions I had about being in a place where perhaps we didn't belong or weren't welcome.

I made my bed, had a shower, donned khaki shorts and a singlet, and prepared to start the day. Things seemed a little better in the light of day. After breakfast we left the house at 7:00 a.m. and got five minutes down the road (distance is only measured in time) when Steve had to turn around and go back as he'd forgotten the tow ropes. These were required as we would be travelling off road and through a lot of rivers.

We left the bitumen just past Kieta Airport (where I'd been told not to go on my own) and cut through country so remote that, according to Steve, "many tribes had never seen a white man". Throughout the course of the day we travelled over 320 kilometres of the roughest terrain I'd ever seen, and way off the beaten track.

Because it was Sunday, everyone was out, some walking to church in their bright 'Sundy-go-meetin' clothes, of sarongs, lap-laps and various clothing in the most vivid colour combinations. There weren't many smiles but hundreds of delayed waves. Many wanted a lift in Steve's flash car. Apparently "the third best on the island".

These people were untouched by Western ways and completely tribal before BCL came along. Steve described the simplicity of life, where children played by simply rolling a stone along the ground with a stick. Now there were transistor radios and old cars everywhere. It was nothing to see a standard Ute with up to twenty people sitting or standing up in the back, all sticking out of the tray like a porcupine.

The Jungles of Bougainville ~ 1983 ~

Along the roadsides, nationals carried large black umbrellas, and many of the women and children smoked pipes. Some people carried huge banana leaves as umbrellas to shelter them from the sun and rain.

The further we went, the denser and darker the vegetation became. There was a pungent smell of leaves rotting on the jungle floor and I could almost taste the warm humidity of the air as I breathed it in. Mingled with this was the occasional whiff of wood smoke, possibly from village huts deep in the jungle.

We passed drum houses along the roadsides. These sacred ritual places were for men only, and were used for ceremonies such as male initiations, and a wide variety of communications. These were constructed as large, thatched roof shelters, above four or six tree trunk supports.

I was able to ascertain that inside were garamuts (slit drums), carved from felled trees or hollowed-out logs, and highly decorated with pigment and carved images. These were their most important instruments. Another was the kundu, an hourglass-shaped drum made of wood with a handle placed on its narrowest part, and snake or lizard skin as a membrane.

The Papuan people understood the drums sound as its 'voice'. This voice carried long distances to announce meetings, call individuals, issue warnings and even contact neighbouring villages. Communication occurred through a complex series of rhythms and tones, beaten out with a wooden stick by an initiated man. More than just an instrument, apart from its rhythmic qualities, each drum was central to the lives of the entire community. They were used as war drums, and to communicate a wide variety of practical messages in rituals of rank, daily life, births and deaths, and would likely include the arrival of strangers.

The World is Your Pearl

As we went deeper into the jungle, Steve rekindled my fears by saying that occasionally there were bandits with machetes or a shotgun who would block the road and hold people up for money. "Oh great!"

We pressed on. The day was getting hotter and very steamy. The scenery was magnificent with strangling vegetation growing everywhere. There were thousands of tall coconut and sago palms, mango, guava, banana and betel nut trees. Beautiful wild orchids, bougainvillea, staghorns and vines ran over everything and dripped from the trees. Strangely though, I saw no wildlife. No roadkill, no birds to speak of.

We passed landslides on a regular basis and areas where the road had been completely washed away by the raging rapids of flooding rivers which sent huge boulders crashing through in their wake and altering the topography in an everlasting bid to confuse.

At one point the road crossed a deep canyon with a thousand-foot drop on either side. The road had eroded so badly that there must have been literally inches to spare for vehicles to get across. I made the mistake of asking Steve to stop for a photo, which he did, right in the middle of it. My heart did backflips as I looked down, seeing nothing but air, to a tiny river which seemed like kilometres below. I closed my eyes and willed us out of there while screaming "keep going, keep going". That was one photograph I'd have to miss.

We must have made at least thirty river crossings, twenty of which we had to drive through. Fortunately for me, because Bougainville was currently experiencing a drought, the rivers were only up to the tops of the wheels at most. Though we did lift our bags and shoes off the floor in anticipation of an indoor paddle a couple of times.

There were several remnants of the Japanese occupation of Bougainville during WWII. We saw Admiral Yamamoto's Mitsubishi

The Jungles of Bougainville ~ 1983 ~

bomber plane wreck, covered with vegetation where it stood in the jungle about three kilometres off the east coast road to the south of Arawa. It was about 25 kilometres north of Buin. This iconic relic lay rusting amongst the vines which undulated everywhere within the deep pockmarks of bomb craters, so deep we could stand up in them.

Admiral Yamamoto was famous as the mastermind behind the attack on Pearl Harbor in Hawaii. He was shot down here by US fighter planes on April 18, 1943. Many other terrestrial WWII relics littered the island, including several tanks and other aeroplanes, as well as sunken boats offshore.

We arrived at Buin where we cruised up and down looking for Charlie, a national who had gone back to his tribe from Panguna to stay with his people for the Saturday. Steve had told him that we would pick him up between 8:00 a.m. and 9:00 a.m. on Sunday morning at the marketplace. However, after having had a good look around, there was no sign of Charlie, so, deciding he must have found a lift back with someone else, we cut out on a narrow jungle path towards the Buin beach where we had a clear view of the Solomon Islands.

Steve pointed upwards, reminding me of the warning about falling coconuts as we were standing directly under fully laden trees which were around 60 feet high. "They'll kill you if you're hit on the head."

We were standing on concrete platforms next to a rusted cannon. An expat who married a national and lived in one of the remote villages we'd passed through, told Steve that one of his children found a skeleton in the jungle where he lived. It still had the helmet sitting on the skull, and the remains of a rifle, minus the wooden butt which had long since rotted away.

We ate fresh pineapple which Liz had cut up to bring along, and drank Sprite lemonade and tonic water, then left the beach and continued inland once again. Resting here and there in rivers, we sat on rocks where the rapids cooled our feet.

Liz talked about cannibalism. There was a story about the first priest who arrived in Buka. He was killed and eaten. They couldn't understand why his feet were so chewy and tough. They were eating his shoes.

History shows that warfare had been common across Bougainville in pre-European times. Groups of residential hamlets formed fighting units of variable composition depending on male leadership contingencies. In the regions of Buin, Buka and some of North Bougainville, leadership was hereditary, but mostly it was based on feats, such as giving feasts for large aggregations of people. In Buka and the far north of Bougainville, the victors engaged in cannibalism, while headhunting was common in the south.

Liz also described that, with the opening of BCL, highlanders from mainland Papua New Guinea would come across to Bougainville on one-way tickets, paid for by the pooling of money from their villages, and with a view to making money. However, they were unqualified, unemployable squatters who found once they arrived, they couldn't get work, but stayed anyway as they had no money to get back. They became rebels who resorted to stealing food and money from wherever and whoever they could get it, in order to live.

As we passed through every river, Steve and Liz related a different hair-raising story of the last time they did this trip at the peak of the rainy season when the rivers were in full flood. They'd navigated raging rapids to the deafening sound of large rocks crashing downstream as they went out one night after receiving word that one of Steve's workmates had lost his car in the river miles from Panguna. The message was relayed to Steve via the mission radio to Horst, the helicopter pilot who notified Steve's friend, Arthur Perry, at BCL.

The Jungles of Bougainville ~ 1983 ~

Arthur, Steve and Liz left Panguna after a long shift at 8:00 p.m. and got back at 6:00 a.m. the next day, just in time to have a shower, eat at the mess and start work again at 7:00 a.m. Like I said, these guys worked hard and played hard! Their mate was grateful that they were able to winch the car out of the river and tow it back to Panguna. Liz said these events happened a lot. Sometimes people could be stuck for days waiting for help. Steve said that trip was very hairy. A wild event, where the car sometimes acted as a submarine. The sort of unforgettable experience he expected to eventually tell his grandchildren.

We travelled for another three hours through very rough, bumpy areas and arrived back at Panguna, to the vast area of the Bougainville copper mine which cut a swathe through the jungle.

There were mountains of slurry (crushed rock waste). Beside it was a river of pale-grey silt which flowed from the mine, and ran for 14 kilometres down through the gorge and spread to a width of a kilometre out to the sea. This grey delta was once the Jaba River.

The mine was a large physical scar on the landscape which implicated a deeper spiritual one in its early days for the people of the communities whose entire way of life was intensely affected. An immense 150,000 tonnes of rock waste and toxic tailings were spewed out, causing rivers to become dead zones.

Steve showed me around. As we drove in, he explained the weight carried by the massive B150 and B170 dump trucks, and told me that if I was driving, not to hesitate in their path as they would never be able to stop suddenly. Everything was enormous. Each dump truck alone looked like the size of a small house.

We saw the Drive House which housed the mountainous stock pile of rock. Steve worked at the B60 crushing plant. It was like hell. I've had previous nightmares about such places. We donned yellow

The World is Your Pearl

helmets and climbed the metal stairs to the top, then walked out on a mesh walkway to the crane. It was a giant horizontal moving platform which was a mechanical device moving back and forth across the crushing plant 60 feet above the vibrating conveyor belts carrying tons of rock.

The crushing plant was very, very noisy, dusty and 'high'. It was a vertigo sufferer's nightmare. I clung to the rail like a limpet, while Steve gave me the full verbal tour at a yell so he could be heard over the din. When the crane arrived at the opposite end, we were positioned above a massive conical funnel into which the reversing trucks tipped their loads of rock. It was terrifying. A handy disposal unit for mafia men!

As we returned to the start, I was glad to get off to climb down the stairs with trembling legs, and get back to the car.

Steve was very adaptable. He was never required to use his welding skills but was made responsible for the mechanical operation of the overhead cranes, which he kept ticking over meticulously. If there was a breakdown, it was up to him to call in the troops to work 36 hours if necessary to get the thing up and running. For every minute of non-operation the cost to the company could be up to $100,000 back then.

This job was often 'all on' or 'all off' which meant that between jobs there was a lot of down time, which Steve utilised by studying for his pilot's licence.

Back outside, Steve took my picture next to one of the dump trucks. I stood by its wheel and only came up to the hub cap!

We left the mine site and drove up to the "best house on the island" which turned out to be the home built for Sir Roderick Carnegie when he was the managing director of BCL. He no longer used it,

The Jungles of Bougainville ~ 1983 ~

though it still operated for VIP banquet functions, cocktail parties and smorgasbords. It mostly sat vacant, looked after by Steve's friend Rod, who was the caretaker and who also took extra care of the 'bar'. He invited us in and mixed us gin and tonics. Very welcome after the long trip and tour of the crushing plant!

Liz showed me through the house. Upstairs were beautiful bedrooms with armchairs, carved tables and subdued lighting. Each bedroom had an ensuite. Each ensuite had an individual tiny courtyard, set with a sunken Roman bath with brass railings. All were exquisitely micro landscaped with stones and tropical plants. I was enchanted with the privilege of seeing it all.

Throughout the rooms were solid wooden cupboards with heaters inside to keep clothes dry and to keep the myriad of luxurious sheets and towels from becoming mildewed and musty in the humidity.

The huge bar downstairs was stocked with everything, including Orrefors and Waterford crystal glasses and decanters. The kitchen had huge cookers and storerooms full of bone china dinnerware, more crystal, and Le Creuset casserole and cookware for the banquet functions. This house had been a real treat to see. We chatted for another hour before returning to Panguna.

Everything to do with the mine site was BIG! We entered the miner's mess hall which was a vast labyrinth of tables and chairs. Trays of food stretched as far as the eye could see in an array of hot soups, roasted meats and vegetables, casseroles, pastas, cold meats, fish, salads, tropical fruits, cakes and slices, cheeses, condiments, apple pies and desserts with cream and custard, freshly squeezed tropical juices, tea and freshly brewed coffee.

The chefs worked in shifts around the clock to feed the hundreds of mine staff who filed through from their own shifts, day and night. Steve introduced me to one of the guys who was eating there as his 'twin' sister. The guy said, "Crikey, mate, what happened to you? Were you hit by a steamroller?"

After dinner we went to the cricket club for a drink before heading back to Arawa to the leave-house. This was just my first day.

The next morning we called at the medical centre. I waited in the car. Steve went in to speak to the doctor who asked what seemed to be the problem? Steve said, "I think I've got malaria." The doctor asked what his symptoms were. Steve said, "My sister's visiting from Australia." Steve arrived back at the car with a medical certificate for a few days off. The doc was pretty good like that. He'd write out a certificate even if someone wanted to go fishing.

I had some wonderful experiences on Bougainville. Driving all over the island visiting pristine beaches with miles of white sand, swaying coconut palms, and plantations of cocoa and copra. One of these was the Numa Numa plantation, the biggest in the Southern Hemisphere. It employed between 2000 and 4000 plantation workers from mainland New Guinea at various times and was so big it managed its affairs through its own bank and post office.

Steve took me up on helicopter flights to see jungles, villages and plantations from above. One flight was heart-stopping. The pilot was Horst. I think he must have been a bit crazy, because we flew directly towards the face of a mountain at speed. I braced myself for impact, when suddenly I felt a heavy gravitational force as we accelerated straight UP. My stomach and brain lurched. When I opened my eyes there was nothing below us. The land seemed to have dropped away to kilometres below us. Always the cool customer, Steve seemed unfazed. But this was another terrifying experience I would never forget.

We visited little islands by boat. I spent time with some children on a small fishing pontoon on one island, and became the object of

The Jungles of Bougainville ~ 1983 ~

raucous laughter by the women on another as I walked through a jungle food market in Buka. I stood out like a sore thumb amongst the nationals.

The market was a huge shelter in the jungle, comprising four poles holding up a large thatched roof above tables of coconuts, breadfruits, avocados, aibika, choko, pumpkin tips, galip nuts, and a variety of tropical fruits, vegetables and live mud crabs, bound up with twine.

We visited the small village where Liz's family lived on Buka Island. They were terribly poor, with hardly any food due to the drought, but very hospitable, offering us breadfruit. We shared the meat from the crab Steve bought from the market. I gave them a bag of my clothes which I'd brought from home to donate to anyone who might need them. Though I wasn't sure if they could or would wear them in this steamy tropical heat.

We continued on to Kessa on the northern tip of Buka Island and swam in the sea. Huge shells sat amongst the sand along the shoreline, perfect and untouched.

Driving north, we went to the tip of Bougainville and across to a tiny island called Sohano, so small we could walk around it in about half an hour. We had to leave the car and cross the water on a ferry to get there.

Sohano Island was another paradise where we stayed overnight in a little guest house called Buka Luma Lodge, a family-run accommodation with a few rooms to one side of a central communal area. Comfortable easy chairs, couches and a single refectory table looked out over a small balcony with cushioned alcoves and beyond to a view of the beautiful waters of the Buka passage.

A chopper pilot was also staying there. His name was Gene. He was about to deliver some explosives to another island and invited

The World is Your Pearl

me to join him for part of the trip. He was not supposed to take passengers whilst carrying volatile explosives in the helicopter; however, things were very flexible in these remote parts in the 1980s. He would drop me in a location to wait for him to make the delivery, then pick me up on his return.

As I climbed in, Gene gave firm instructions that when I exited, I must ensure the seatbelt was secure and not to slam the door on it. He started the ignition and up we went, over the jungle, swooping down on crocodiles swimming in the rivers, dipping to see war wrecks, and eventually we descended to where he dropped me somewhere in a compound to wait for him to return. I had headphones on, but as we landed, his information and instructions cut out. I had no idea where I was, nor the dynamics of the people I may encounter. Nervously, I jumped out, slamming the door on the seatbelt. "Bugger."

I was wearing a singlet and shorts, and all I carried was my large Minolta camera. Remembering the 'sticky situation' warnings from my boss, Mike Buxton, and backed up by my husband, I began to panic.

An ancient old man wandered through the jungle clearing, carrying a long spear. He stopped and stared at me as though I was an alien from outer space.

My heart pumped with panic as I walked with purpose past some official-looking buildings and down to the shoreline where an embankment shielded me from anyone who may have been able to see me. I sat down behind it with my hand over my watch so I couldn't see the time tick by in slow motion, and worked out my strategies in case any attackers should come out of the jungle. I could run into the sea, but my camera would get wet. I could try to outrun them, but they had spears.

The Jungles of Bougainville ~ 1983 ~

I'm not sure how long I was sitting there, freaking out in a cold sweat, when suddenly I looked up. Sixty feet above me soared a fully laden coconut tree. What should I do? Do I hedge my bets and move out from behind the embankment which shielded me from view, and on to the open beach? Do I chance the people from the buildings seeing, and possibly coming down to 'get' me? Or do I hope a coconut doesn't fall?

Suddenly, 'THWACK', the decision was made for me, as a huge coconut dropped from above and embedded itself in the sand right next to me. I crouched down and edged along the embankment, just as I heard the distant sound of the chopper returning. I ran back to the landing pad where Gene picked me up. In my nervy state, I slammed the door on the seat belt. "Bloody hell" I did it again. As we took off into the air I was on the brink of tears. Trying not to show my upset, I couldn't speak all the way back.

Later that afternoon, Gene joined us for gin and tonics on the veranda. Steve asked him where he'd left me. Gene explained that he had dropped me at a local government station, the friendliest place on the island. It turned out that if I had found any of the authorities, they would have treated me like a queen. But no one came to greet me as they probably thought I was a missionary. It was sad that no one knew I was there as I hid on the beach, terrified.

After more gin and tonics, Steve found some snorkel gear for Gene and the three of us, and we wandered down to the water, where, with no alternative route, we crunched our way across the coral to a drop-off.

Since writing this book, in all my years of travel through hundreds of world destinations, the best experience I've ever had was this time I spent with my brother in Bougainville, and the jewel within the jewel was an extraordinary experience of mind-blowing wonderment, where for the next two hours we were carried along the most exquisite coral reef by the sea current.

This concentration of reef life sat one foot from our faces as we peered into and around things. We were entering a kaleidoscope of vivid colours within the silent and private world of a myriad of creatures as they went about their daily lives. This was indescribable. No documentary by Jacques Cousteau or David Attenborough could show what we experienced, because we were there.

Amongst thousands of the most intensely coloured corals and seaweeds were millions of what seemed to be fluorescent sea creatures, twinkling in every colour, pattern and shape imaginable.

Fish in their thousands flashed and glittered around us. There were shrimps, shellfish, crabs, octopuses, sea cucumbers, seahorses, stonefish and intensely blue starfish. Bright sea anemones in dazzlingly vivid colour combinations were mesmerising as they swayed in the current with their accompanying clownfish swimming inside them. An occasional black crown-of-thorns starfish fed on the coral.

At one point I watched a black-and-white-striped sea snake with a yellow head wind its way around my leg and swim away. Gene tugged on my foot and beckoned me up. Above the water he told me that it was one of the most venomous creatures on earth and if it had bitten me, I wouldn't have reached the shore. However, I wasn't bitten and was having the time of my life in complete euphoria. It was like a dream I never wanted to end.

I have searched the world for such a concentration of reef life ever since in the hope of experiencing something like it again, but nothing has even come close.

The following day, travelling back through the jungle, we were hit by a violent tropical storm. The ford we were about to cross

The Jungles of Bougainville ~ 1983 ~

was covered by a tsunami of water which crashed down along the course of the river in a torrential wall of water, bringing large rocks and boulders and a huge tree trunk in its wake. The tree trunk lodged itself between the concrete ford and the rocks beneath it. This powerful force of surging water pushed it vertical, causing an avalanche of water to spew upwards and cascade out on either side. This was a phenomenal sight, a spectacular display of pure drama from Mother Nature herself. It was an image which stuck in my brain forever—too wet and wild to take a photograph.

We waited in the Hilux until almost dark before the water subsided enough for us to pass. Some missionaries came down to see if we'd like to come and wait it out in their huts, but Steve politely declined. I often wondered what their digs would have been like, but I knew Steve wouldn't have left his vehicle unattended in these parts. It was treacherous for so many reasons.

Years later, in 2012, there was a movie released called *Mr. Pip*. It was based on the book of the same name by Lloyd Jones and starred Hugh Laurie. The plot was set in 1989:

MISTER PIP:-

~ As civil war raged on in the province of Bougainville, then called North Solomons, in Papua New Guinea. Mr. Watts, the only white man left on the island after a blockade, reopens the local school. The 'Redskins', an army sent to destroy the local rebels, are getting closer ~

The movie was beautifully filmed but ended in shocking violence. It rocked me to the core, ending as this sweet, gentle teacher was attacked, chopped up with machetes and fed to the pigs. It stayed with me, unleashing the unease I'd felt when I first arrived. The later knowledge of how hated the white men must have been.

The World is Your Pearl

This movie described one story. But I came away with the further knowledge of what had been done.

The slurry I'd described earlier, flowing into the Jaba delta, was a silt of tailings from the mine. A toxic waste of chemical destruction which ran through what used to be abundant farmland and a freshwater river alive with fish, now lay waste. The tribesmen who lived on the lowlands were displaced and had to move to higher ground into other tribal territories where they didn't belong.

For many of the people, their land had been destroyed by BCL. The only dwellers who lived there now were crocodiles. The people's way of life was gone forever. There was never much compensation to the people of Bougainville, as the wealth in dollars and millions of kina went to mainland PNG to develop cities, and build highways into the highlands and other mine sites.

Having said this, the good things which came to Bougainville as a result of BCL during the mine's life between 1972 and 1989 were health services and education. As well, around 12,000 people were trained, including approximately 1,000 who completed full-trade apprenticeships and some 400 who completed graduate and post-graduate studies. During the mine's construction and development phase the demand for goods and services was in part met by the local community and this demand helped foster the development of various local enterprises.

The organisation of the mine's food-buying requirements, for example, through rural consolidated agencies opened up a lucrative market for garden-style cash crops.

Ancillary services functions also created new opportunities for local contractors in areas such as the provision of labour, transport, construction and security. Through the Bougainville Development Corporation there was also a focus on the fostering of mid-sized

The Jungles of Bougainville ~ 1983 ~

ventures. Its areas of initiative included air services, steel fabrication, catering services, furniture manufacturing and livestock processing.

These days, leaders in the ABG (Autonomous Bougainville Government), and even external advisors, want to see the reopening of the Panguna mine as an impact project to kick-start the Bougainville economy. This once-lucrative open-cut mine has been abandoned for more than two decades and would need an estimated $8 to $10 billion investment to restart it. In addition to operational costs, any restart at Panguna would have to deal with demands for compensation from locals and expectations of an environmental clean-up around the mine site.

The possibility of conflict is a serious one considering the large number of weapons still on the island and the highly factionalised population.

Everywhere one travels in Bougainville these days there is urban decay, pothole-infested public roads and streets, fearful squatter settlements, massive unemployment, crime and an Asian takeover of cottage businesses.

If not for the BCL copper mine, I would never have seen this beautiful place or even really known of its existence. But I often wonder what it was like there before the 1970s when the tribal people lived their simple lives in the jungle.

If Steve was alive today and I thought it possible to return with any safety I'd go back without hesitation. Even in Bougainville's now derelict state, it must surely have returned to an organic abundance.

A trip into the wilds of anywhere beats the hell out of tourism any day as long as you're with someone savvy. This had been one of the wildest adventures I've ever had. There wasn't a minute when I hadn't felt safe in Steve's hands, and with never a dull moment.

CHAPTER 2

A Lucky Escape—Bali ~ 2002 ~

There are people whose lives can be changed in a matter of seconds by others who don't even know them.

Pete and I were divorcing after 24 years of marriage. It was an emotional nightmare for both of us. Cameron was 19, Emma was 17. Both old enough to (sort of) deal with it.

Cameron had moved out of home. Emma and I purchased backpacks and travelled through Italy for a month from late March 2002. Then, at Emma's suggestion, we took off again in late September for a more relaxing holiday in Bali, and had a ball.

It was just what we needed. 'Girl time' without the hard slog of carrying a huge backpack. Sun, beaches, massages, manicures, pedicures, good food and 'shopping'.

The World is Your Pearl

We stayed in a beautiful resort bungalow, right on the beach in Kuta. While having a drink at the poolside cocktail bar, we met Tess, also an artist, and also going through a divorce. She was from Brisbane on holiday with her son and daughter. We caught up quite often and shared a driver a couple of times to explore the island. Tess was fragile as her divorce was from a violent husband. She was also a very gentle, spiritual soul; she was tuned in to the Universe and humbly described herself as quite psychic.

One night we headed off to the Sari Club. There weren't many people there as it was only 9:00 p.m., so it was surprising to see several uniformed security guards out the front. A bit of overkill, we thought. We walked through and ordered our drinks at the bar. Tess tapped me on the shoulder and said, "Glenda, I'm really sorry, but do you think we could go somewhere else? I just have to get out of here." I said, "Sure" and cancelled our drinks order and beckoned Emma to leave.

Emma was confused and said, "Mum, I really wanted to come to the Sari Club." I told her Tess didn't want to stay and not to worry as they were leaving in the morning and we could come back tomorrow night.

From there we headed to Paddy's Bar. We ordered beers but Tess didn't want to be there either. So we finished our drinks in a hurry and headed down the road to the Apache Bar for some food before exchanging contact details and saying goodbye.

The following day we met a really fun group from a couple of resorts along the beach and they wanted to join us at the Sari Club that night. The place was packed. Emma danced all night with some spunky guys up the back and I drank a lot of jungle juice, a rough grog distilled by the locals, and talked to people all night. We had a ball and laughed all the way home at four o'clock in the morning.

A Lucky Escape—Bali ~ 2002 ~

Some people sitting around the pool the next day greeted us with a chuckle and asked if we'd had a good time the night before. Needless to say, that day was to be a quiet veg-out day by the pool.

The following day we travelled up to Langsat Village and went white water rafting down the Telaga Waja River past steep rice paddies, through steamy lush jungles with little thatched huts amongst dripping vines, and where people washed in the river. As we floated along the less turbulent areas with moments to contemplate, I could glimpse the real lives of the Balinese. Their lifestyle seemed quiet, simple and gentle. The people have very little, but are rich in the absence of Western clutter, though I would love to see a balance where they had a little more and we had less.

We stopped under a waterfall and marvelled at a kingfisher flashing its shimmering electric blue feathers in the sunlight, then swept off again down the river for a long time, sometimes gliding, sometimes churning over rapids, to a place where we dropped four metres over a dam wall.

Gripping the ropes with white knuckles, we screamed with laughter and relief at the finale of what had been two hours of fun-filled activity.

At the end , some local women were waiting by the river to deflate and fold the rafts. They carried them on their heads up the same steep track that we were struggling to climb.

In the breeze at the top of a high cliff, we enjoyed a delicious lunch from a buffet of fragrant rice dishes, salads and tropical fruits. It was like a dream. Sitting in the steamy heat of the jungle in an open thatched dining area, we ate amidst the chirrup of insects, while looking out over the river winding far below.

The next day was spent on a Bali Hai Reef Cruise where a catamaran took us to Lembongan Island to visit a tiny village with

The World is Your Pearl

its various small wood carving industries, then out into the bay in a submersible submarine to see fish and coral, to the distorted tunes of The Beatles' 'We All Live in a Yellow Submarine'. We returned to the catamaran for a sumptuous lunch before going out again for banana boat rides, water slides and snorkelling.

Back in Kuta, on the beach and throughout the many stalls along Poppies Lane, we enjoyed a huge amount of banter, bartering with the local sellers and stallholders, shopping for 'designer' t-shirts, sarongs, shell jewellery and trinkets.

Purchasing Kentucky Fried Chicken for lunch one day, I kept the scraps for the skinny local dogs. As I pulled them out later to feed them, a lady walked up and said, "Can I look?" She asked to have the bits which still had some meat on them. It broke my heart.

We returned home from Bali on October 6, 2002. While sitting up in bed having a cup of tea six days later on October 12, I was listening to the radio news. My ears pricked up. Bali bombing! Sari Club! Paddy's Bar!

I picked up the phone and called Tess in Brisbane. Had she heard the news? When we were there, she hadn't been able to explain the terrible sense of doom and dread she'd felt while we were in the Sari Club.

While ordering our drinks, she'd gone to the bar to order a rum and coke, but she said she was overwhelmed by such a feeling of *sheer terror* that the words wouldn't come out to order the drink. She'd never experienced anything like it before, but could only describe it as 'pure evil'.

Two bombs had been detonated during one of the busiest tourist periods of the year in Kuta Beach. One was from a backpack-mounted suicide bomber inside Paddy's Bar. Then 20 seconds

A Lucky Escape—Bali ~ 2002 ~

later, a much more powerful car bomb, hidden inside a Mitsubishi van, was detonated by another suicide bomber outside the Sari Club. At the same time, a third, much smaller device was detonated outside the American Consulate in Denpasar.

I later read a report that the bombings were in direct retaliation for support of the United States' war on terror and Australia's role in the liberation of East Timor. Tragically, 202 people, including 88 Australians, died horrific deaths, and a further 209 people were seriously injured.

The repercussions rippled through the Balinese community for many years. They relied so much on the tourism industry which dropped away as a result.

In April 2004, at the age of 19, Emma went back to the Indonesian isle, to aid the Balinese in their continuing time of need. With her longing to be a midwife, she gathered donations of vitamins, Spirulina health formula, breast pumps, baby rugs and funds for medical supplies, and volunteered to spend three months helping an American midwife who was devoting her life to helping Balinese women give birth safely.

The midwife, known as Ibu Robin, had set up the Yayasan Bumi Sehat Healthy Mother, Healthy Baby Foundation, and for many years ran a rural clinic, delivering babies to mothers who couldn't afford to give birth in hospitals.

Em lived in a compound with Ibu Robin and her family in a village near Ubud.

They travelled on a motorbike in all weathers, often in the middle of the night, attending to the women whose circumstances were very different, sometimes giving birth on just a plastic tablecloth on the dirt floor of a hut.

The World is Your Pearl

Sadly, Emma only got to stay for one month, due to visa issues, but in that life-changing time, she assisted with the births of 10 babies.

CHAPTER 3

The Human Snow Plough—Perisher ~ 2005 ~

"Inky sapphires, watery aquamarines and glacial diamonds. Dive in and indulge"
ART: is precise, permanent, meticulous, inside the lines. Even the most outrageous scrawl is usually well thought out in advance.
LIFE: on the other hand is transient, fleeting, messy. It doesn't care if it strays outside the lines—(unknown).

My brother and I always had fun together. He flew down from the Gold Coast with his mate Wally, and Wally's wife Cheryl. I flew up from Melbourne and we met in Canberra. We took a bus to the Perisher ski fields, where Cheryl had organised a private ski lodge for us, called Chez Juan.

The World is Your Pearl

Steve, Wally and Cheryl

Steve, Wally and Cheryl had skied together for many years in Australia, Canada and on the Italian alps. They each did their own things. Steve and Wally attacked the black slopes and Cheryl stuck to the places she was comfortable in. I was to be sent to the baby slopes on my own for three days of ski lessons.

Early the next morning, Cheryl cooked breakfast. A huge slap-up affair of bacon, sausages, baked beans, tomatoes, eggs, toast, marmalade and brewed coffee.

Well fortified, we headed down to hire my skis, poles, boots, locker, ski racks and to organise ski lessons and mountain tow passes. I arranged to have all my lessons over on Perisher Smiggins, where it was more sheltered and not so steep to start off. By the time I got the bus across to Smiggins and walked in, my feet had blistered from the hired boots.

The Human Snow Plough—Perisher ~ 2005 ~

Half a pack of Band-Aids later I was with the beginners group. There were eight of us with a marvellous Canadian instructor called Shaun Fleming. He was very calm and relaxed, talking me through every move, calling down the slope "Relax, Glenda … think beautiful thoughts … think flowers and roses …!!"

Within two hours he had us tapping out the snow from our boots, fitting the skis, walking pigeon-toed, ski-over-ski through snow, skiing on one ski, then the other, jumping off the snow, springing up, turning right using the left foot in an arrow then left using right, and snow ploughing to a stop. When we were confident with all that we were taken up the hill on the T-bar to ski to the bottom. I couldn't have had a better ski instructor. He made me forget all about my badly blistered feet.

After the lesson, I headed back to Perisher on the bus. Cheryl found me sitting in the sun having a beer. We found Steve and Wally at the lockers where I was refitted with a different pair of boots, stowed everything and headed home for well-earned drinks and nibbles to celebrate our first day, as we looked out over the frosty trees and mountain-top views.

We ate lasagne by the open fire. Then, dosed up on painkillers for my ankles with lots of flesh missing due to the ill-fitting boots, I was cosy in bed by 8:00 p.m. with a blizzard raging outside.

The next morning the second pair of ski boots were even worse. My lesson only lasted half an hour before I had to limp back for yet another change of boots. My feet were a mess and I was in agony. I told Shaun I had to give it away for the day. He said to rest and soak my feet. So I stowed my new boots and the readjusted skis and headed off to the Blue Cow for a beer and something to eat.

Sitting in the window I did some sketches of the vast snow-capped mountain range, some drawings of people in their crazy hats and one of the snow plough parked below me. I spent the rest of the afternoon reading my book in the bar then headed home for a bath and to put salve on my ankles. Steve and Wally cooked a lovely Italian pasta dinner, opened a nice bottle of red wine and we dug in for the night.

After a hot breakfast and lots of brewed coffee, we all went to Smiggins on the bus. My ankle wounds, which were open and fleshy, were slathered with salve, strapped and padded with surgical plasters, and, with extra socks in the third pair of hired boots, I was ready to hit the slopes. Steve took me for two runs to the top on the chairlift and down both sides to gain confidence before the lesson. This pair of boots were 'back closing' and turned out to be great. Third time lucky.

I went to the meeting place for a coffee before the lesson and ended up having a Canadian Club whiskey with the others at the bar. A little Dutch courage before the lesson must have done the trick. I met Shaun and the others and took the chairlift to the top and skied beautifully down ten times. I was ready to join Steve, Wally and Cheryl on the slopes.

Steve and Wally met me for another Canadian Club whiskey, before we took the T-bar up to the top of the mountain. There was a blizzard and conditions over the ridge were bad. I skied in terror. Having been used to miles of slope in every direction, this was a 'trail' with markers and 'edges' to fall over.

I nervously inched my way, as little kids whisked past me with the greatest of ease. Steve and Wally were very patient with my tentative snow-ploughing efforts. I got around the slope to a downhill run, when suddenly I was out of control! I flew past Wally, then Steve. Wally said, "Gee she's doing well." I was flying downhill in angel gear, and when I hit Steve's arm as I went past at 80 miles an hour he knew there was something wrong.

The Human Snow Plough—Perisher ~ 2005 ~

I stayed upright for a long time, controlling the moves, building up speed, still in angel gear. When I threw the stocks up in the air Steve knew then that there was definitely something wrong. I became airborne and hit the snow face first. I was laughing so hard under the snow I couldn't get up. Steve had to dig my ski goggles out of the snow. I'd packed them into the ice with my face! The three of us were aching with laughter as they went about gathering up skis, stocks and beanie.

Steve pointed back to the tip of a rock jutting out of the snow, several feet from where I'd landed. I could have lost my face or head or broken my neck! Possibly ended up in a wheelchair for life. That took the smiles off our faces for a second or two. But all was well, and off we went once again heading downhill.

This time down a narrow track between two large bodies of ice-water ponds. I made it through to where we took the Intercepter (chairlift) right to the top. We all hopped on together with me in the middle. Steve said, "Now, get your backside as close as you can towards the front of the seat, then when you get off, just ski forward. There are no angles to navigate. But don't muck about or you'll be in the way of the next people getting off behind you."

"Okay."

At the right moment we all got off. Steve and Wally skied forwards; however, when I left the chairlift, my skis landed on solid ice and went from under me. The back of my head hit the ice with such force, Steve said the sound was like a watermelon being hit with a hammer. He knew it was serious when I let out a low groan. I knew it was serious when I felt the blood pouring down my back in a warm river.

The World is Your Pearl

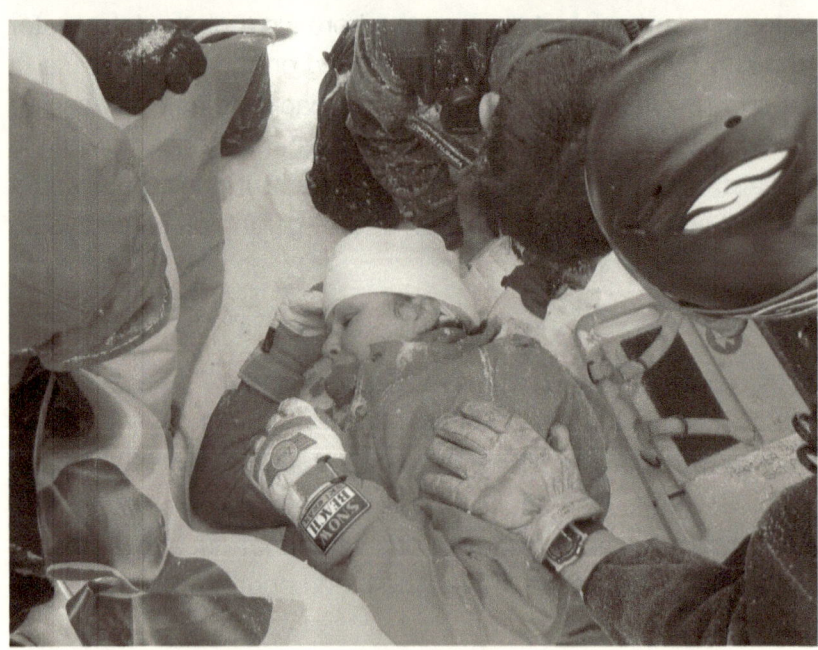

Perisher rescue

The Human Snow Plough—Perisher ~ 2005 ~

I couldn't move out of the way as people were falling over each other as they came off the chairlift. It became very dangerous and eventually they stopped the chairlift. I'm not sure how long the whole rescue took, but I've often thought back and wondered about all the poor people sitting so high up, swinging in the blizzard weather.

Someone made a pillow of snow under my head and six men made a shield around me, hunkered on their knees and linking arms at their shoulders like a pod. They kept talking to me, saying, "Are you still with us?" Telling sick jokes, anything they could think of.

A medical officer from the ski patrol arrived. He sounded Irish but turned out to be Japanese learning English in Canada! He bandaged my head and I was put on a board and strapped tightly with Velcro, then lifted into a trailer behind a Ski-Doo and bumped away as I was transported down the mountain to the start of the tube railway at the Blue Cow. I was wheeled onto the last carriage of the train where I lay in front of the legs and ski stocks of people commuting.

I was wheeled out onto the platform at Perisher (rather fitting), and into a lift up to the medical centre. Feeling pretty seedy by now, I was in shock, shaking, had lost lots of blood and badly needed to pee. There was a lot of activity around me. I tried to stand up but started to pass out and grabbed the ambo on the way down. He got me to the loo, at last, as my bladder was out of control. With five X-rays to check for skull fractures, I underwent three to four hours of surgery for a massive hematoma on the skull.

For some reason I was not put under general anaesthetic. Five local anaesthetic needles in my head stung like a bee. I panted through it to deal with the pain as I had for childbirth. The sound of the surgeons squishing inside the gaping two-inch hole in my head was sickening.

The World is Your Pearl

They put me together, with not vinegar and brown paper, but twenty stitches internally and externally. Steve was with me. He took some photos but said he couldn't watch. The assistant had gauze over his finger poking it into the hole in my head. The gauze disappeared, he'd pull it out and get another one. Lots of blood and cold water. They did such a good job, and hardly cut off any of my hair.

With a $340 bill for surgery, and a bandaged head, we left to walk home in the snow.

When we arrived home, Cheryl got me sorted with a shower and PJs and took all my bloodied clothes and washed them. She had a lovely bowl of soup and a hot meal on the table for us. I ate the soup but started to pass out and went to lie on the bed and fell asleep.

Cheryl and Wally went out to dinner. Steve stayed behind with me and I woke and got up later when they returned. Cheryl reheated the rest of my meal for me, and over cups of tea we laughed and laughed over my 'ice facial'.

In our beds that night, Steve and I talked for ages. He told me that when I was taken away down the mountain he wasn't thinking straight. Wally took off to find Cheryl as he expected Steve would go down with me on the back of the Ski-Doo. But the Ski-Doo driver had taken off. Everyone had gone in different directions. Steve found himself skiing a black run in a blizzard, going so fast he was in peril. He suddenly realised he was in danger himself, so slowed down and thought things through. Realising he didn't know where he was going, he simply followed the markers from point to point. The big rule on the slopes is NEVER SKI ALONE, but he'd really thought I was going to die. What a day! Everything turned out okay in the end, and all was well that ended well.

In the following days I felt crook; my body was really banged up, black and blue with bruises, with a nasty one on the left calf muscle,

The Human Snow Plough—Perisher ~ 2005 ~

and my neck went purple from the whiplash. I had bruising also on my hip and waist, every muscle complained when I got up or down, and my head hurt like hell.

It sure took my mind off my sore ankle!

CHAPTER 4

From the Cradle to the Lake ~ March 2006 ~

Tasmanian Overland—100 kilometre walk—Cradle Mountain to Lake St Clair

**And into the forest I go,
to lose my mind and find my soul—John Muir.**

Postcard from Hobart:
"We've done it. Hardest thing I've ever done. We walked well over 100 kilometres with heavy packs. Body screaming with pain. Scenery glorious. Overrun with mice and possums at night. Experienced all weather. Met wonderful strangers and wildlife. Lots of laughs. No blood. Lots of sweat. Some tears.
Loved it but glad it's over. Love Glenda"

had been teaching oil painting, watercolour and drawing at the local Sherbrooke Art Gallery for the past 17 years. Many of my students had become firmly entrenched as lifetime friends.

The World is Your Pearl

One of them was Debra. She worked as a senior nurse in the emergency department at the local William Angliss Hospital in Ferntree Gully. This was the hospital where I was born, as well as my brother, our father before us, his siblings and both my children.

In class one day, Debra spoke of walking the Overland Track from Cradle Mountain to Lake St Clair in Tasmania. From her description, it sounded like a great challenge and a chance to experience an intensely beautiful place on the world heritage wilderness list. It didn't take much discussion for it to become a serious undertaking by a group of seven girls, requiring careful planning, thorough preparation and the essential acquisition of appropriate gear. Emma and I brought out our backpacks once again.

Our group consisted of Deb and her 15-year-old daughter Katie, Keron, a fellow nursing friend of Deb's, myself and my daughter Emma who was 20 years old, a close friend of mine, Claire, who loved an active adventure, and a friend of hers, Christine.

We flew to Launceston and were collected at the airport by our transfer driver, Dennis. As he approached us, we wondered how he knew it was us he needed to collect as he hadn't held up a name sign. He told us he knew we were his group by our "bloody clodhoppin' boots".

Throughout the bus trip to our start point, he gave us a running commentary on the price of hay bales and how many cattle they fed, the height of every mountain, the number of people each hut could accommodate, the rainfall, the people—a constant verbal dialogue which lasted all the way to the visitors centre at Cradle Mountain.

After a stop for food and alcohol provisions and making payments for track fees, hut fees, bus fares, and wondering about the extra 'per person' charge for fuel, we were taken further to the Waldheim

From the Cradle to the Lake ~ March 2006 ~

Chalet huts, which were bare-bones bunkhouse-style camping cabins with bunk beds and simple kitchenettes. This was where we met up with Claire's friend Christine, the seventh member of our group, who had travelled up from her home on the most southern tip of Tasmania near Cygnet.

The Waldheim Chalet itself was built in 1910 by Gustav Weindörfer, an Austrian-born, Australian amateur botanist. He and his wife, Kate, purchased hundreds of acres in the Cradle Mountain Valley and built their chalet from King Billy pine harvested from the adjacent forest.

The Chalet was named Waldorf 'home in the forest' and was built to allow tourists to stay in the valley.

It was late summer, heading for Tasmania's autumn. I'd spent several weeks dehydrating fruit and vegetables for our meals on the trek in an attempt to keep the weight of the packs down. Because the weather is so unpredictable all year round, we were required to carry tents, even though we were to stay in survival huts along the way. Sudden weather changes where fog and clouds can descend without warning can cause a party to become disoriented with no visibility. It can often snow at any time of the year, which meant we needed to take 'everything' for our survival.

Although we packed carefully, considering everything as 'weight' right down to items as small as matches, my pack was 20 kgs. As well as the tent, items included food, clothing, toiletries, stove, cooking fuel, cooking and eating vessels, sleeping mat, sleeping bag, washing facilities, water bottles, camera, and incidentals like playing cards, a small sketchbook and pencils.

The night before we left on day one of our trek, we ate a lavish 'last supper' of roasted meats and vegetables, washed down with red wine. From this meal we were able to set out the next day with a few delicious sandwiches made up from the leftovers.

The World is Your Pearl

After our last shower for nine days, and signing the log book at the start of the track, we left at 8:30 a.m. and walked out through mossy forests.

With our packs fully laden with all food provisions, the heaviest for the entire trip, we traversed the highest ascent of the Overland Track, making the packs seem even heavier.

My body was physically challenged and I was still unsure that I would get used to the rhythm of trekking with a heavy pack. My every footfall was considered with care for fear of turning an ankle, or worse, as the paths were steep and rocky through these glacially carved valleys.

We meandered along a pretty stretch of alpine water called Dove Lake. It was glass smooth, still and silent. Reflecting a deep blue colour from the sky, it mirrored clouds passing overhead. From here we headed along a rocky path towards Marions Lookout where we hauled ourselves up by chains embedded into the vertical rock face.

Emma scarpered up with ease, released her pack, then shimmied back down the cliff to where I was struggling up, not just under the weight of my pack, but with issues of vertigo, which debilitated and shut my brain down. She took my pack to the top, while assisting me at the same time, talking me through, enabling me to focus enough to get control of each move of the climb. What a darling daughter! 'Emma Pearl; What a Girl'!

Over the ridge at the top the views were spectacular. We had an excellent vantage point to see Dove Lake below us, and far beyond to the peaks of Cradle Mountain.

Before she left for Tasmania, Claire's son Neil gave her a present of a little Buddha. It was roughly an inch tall. She carried it in her pocket and photographed it wherever we went, on the tops of cairns and summits throughout the trek.

From the Cradle to the Lake ~ March 2006 ~

We climbed among fragrant eucalypts in fog, mist and clouds and out along boardwalks through button grass moorlands. I could see why our early pioneering botanist was so enchanted with the flora he discovered here. The beauty across the alpine plateau was like rock ponds by the sea. Pools of water known as 'tarns' hosted magnificent mounds of button grasses standing between rocks with lichens which appeared to be painted like jewels of an intensely contrasting patchwork of vivid colour patterns. The button grasses were so named because the yellow flowers which sprouted from their pin cushion foliage were once dried to harden, and used by convicts as buttons.

Walking along boardwalks through the alpine meadows, we ate our only 'luxury' gourmet lunch for the next ten days amongst rock crags on the open plateau, in Kitchen Hut.

Cradle Mountain looked ominous, covered with cloud and mist. We felt cold and took out our plastic coats. However, by the time we got to its base, the sky had totally cleared and the sun came out.

We all left the trail, dumped the packs and started up the mountain. Sadly, I got two-thirds of the way to the summit and was forced to turn back due to vertigo. I have a terrible fear of heights, and a fear of falling. It's a crippling feeling which comes over me when I'm exposed with nothing to hold on to. I reach a point where my mind goes into a form of seizure, and I freeze, unable to move.

As I descended, I was able to take in the view from some spots. Even from this lower altitude the sight was spectacular, like being on top of the world. Everyone else climbed to the top.

On reaching the bottom, I did a few stretching exercises, left a note on Deb's pack to say I'd gone for water, then found a stream and filled the flask.

The World is Your Pearl

When they came down, we all set out for a further three and a half hours of 'hard' walking to the Waterfall Valley Hut. The elements turned again and we were battling strong winds and rain. We did well, though I was in a lot of pain through my feet, ankles, knees, shoulders, neck and back, and it was from this point that I began to require six lots of Nurofen painkillers a day, just to get through the joint pain. I fast discovered that my body was just not built to carry heavy weight over any distance. I must have a selective memory, because Emma and I backpacked around Italy four years ago, and that was pretty hard too. I recalled some extremely tough days, with me ending in tears suffering excruciating pain in my back, feet and ankles.

This had been a steep and tiring 10.4 kilometre climb. I was so eager to get to the hut to relieve myself of the burden of my heavy pack that I burned ahead with the others, not noticing that Deb and Keron had lagged a long way back and were in strife. Keron had cramps and neither of them had any water, as Keron had run out and Katie had been carrying Deb's.

By the time they eventually arrived, they were clearly 'pissed off'.

We all apologised. Everyone was upset and emotional. This had been a bad start. Poor Katie felt terrible as she left with Deb to go and pitch their tent together outside the hut.

All the camping accommodations throughout the valley are very basic, with no electricity. The main one in Waterfall Gully was a wooden survival hut with 24 bunk beds. There was an area to eat, but no cooking facilities or inside toilets. Beside this was another smaller hut, basic with eight bunks. Near every hut along the track, level wooden platforms are available where tents can be pitched above the ground.

We ate our first dinner cooked on Trangias. These are ingenious Swedish-designed lightweight camp stoves fuelled with methanol

From the Cradle to the Lake ~ March 2006 ~

which we carried separately in aluminium flasks. Emma and I ate mushroom soup, rice and dehydrated vegetables. Food for the others varied individually.

It was a bitterly cold night, with howling gale force winds, so wild we thought the hut would be blown away. I thought of Deb and Katie in their tent ... (probably in Windermere by now!).

But despite the pelting rain, their tent survived the night, and it was a new day. After hot porridge and coffee we had help from a volunteer ranger. She gave us tips on how to correctly repack our packs for efficient access, comfort and even weight distribution. Claire had previously done a lot of backpack camp treks, and suggested we use our plastic ponchos as pack covers against the rain.

The morning was cold and overcast. We tramped past little pademelons, like small wallabies, watching us with soaked fur, from where they sat by the pit toilet. Having set out late at 9.45 a.m., we wore plastic coats, pants and gaiters, prepared for bad weather, which we got. The skies were dark and gloomy, and the horizontal, driving rain almost sliced through us as we trudged along.

For just over four hours, we headed towards Windermere Hut. Even though the weather was wet and freezing and we'd walked in rain most of the way, the path underfoot had fewer obstacles. This leg of our journey wasn't strenuous, as we moved easily through enchanting mossy forests, arriving at Lake Windermere around 2:00 p.m. The scenery was spectacular, with glorious ancient pines and low vegetation which looked like a prehistoric garden.

Windermere Hut was similar to the Waterfall Valley Hut with 24 bunk beds, a composting pit toilet and rainwater tank. After settling in, we boiled water to wash, ate a hot lunch and sat around all afternoon, then unwound before dinner with some yoga on the helipad, symbolically bowing to Claire's little Buddha in the centre.

The World is Your Pearl

A few strangers joined in, and amazingly, four of them lived and worked locally back home and we discovered they were connected to us through our own schools, pharmacy and hospital. Of course we were only about 700 kilometres from home, but people came from all over Australia, indeed all over the world, to trek the Overland Track in Tasmania. Throughout my travels, the six degrees of separation never ceases to amaze.

The Overland Track was beautifully maintained and signposted, and the huts were solid enough for survival. Some had basic gas heating which was controlled to when it could be used. Each hut had a rainwater tank, plumbed to sink taps. Luxury!

The next day was a big 17 kilometre walk to Pelion Hut. We were psyched for the worst. Walking was a continuous uphill challenge, as we picked our way over gnarled, tangled and snaking roots which criss-crossed everywhere beneath the dense vegetation. With constant climbs over slippery rocks and stones, we took it easy and kept on, along planks, logs, boardwalks, mud puddles and through streams of running water. Somehow, for me, it wasn't so bad. As I got into the rhythmic pattern of 'foot-mind-eye' coordination, it was like a walking meditation through a sensual wonderland of beauty.

Everywhere rocks and boulders were covered with colourful lichens of electric orange, soft greens, golds and velvety blacks.

We walked on through magnificent mossy forests of fluorescent green trees, flamboyantly dressed in flamenco skirts of dripping mosses which cascaded over each other. Further into the ancient rainforest, some dense areas became so dark it was like Lord of the Rings' Mirkwood.

We passed cascading waterfalls, crossed suspension bridges over rushing rivers and ate lunch by a fast-flowing creek. Later in the

From the Cradle to the Lake ~ March 2006 ~

afternoon we rested by a river beneath a tree so huge we could sit amongst its massive roots.

Beyond the forest, we emerged through beautiful grasslands which billowed across frog flats, so named because of the chorus of many frog sounds, and arrived at Pelion Hut in record time at 4:00 p.m. Once again we enjoyed some yoga on the nearby helipad.

With Claire orchestrating our yoga poses, many strangers from the hut joined in or photographed the spectacle of the large group performing stretches in unison. It was perfect against the backdrop of Mount Oakleigh's dolerite spires, with a glowing sunset sky beyond.

Pelion Hut is the largest of all the alpine huts in the Cradle Mountain-Lake St Clair National Park, with balconies skirting its entire perimeter. These balconies became a social mecca that evening, not only for the people; below them in the grass by the nearby creek were a wombat, a brushtail possum and two pademelons. These were marsupials, native to the area.

We ate our food in a large common area within the hut, which housed bunks for 60 people in six rooms. Each room was a thoroughfare to the next, so it got pretty noisy at night.

It was only an eight kilometre walk the next day to get to Kia Ora Hut, which was nestled next to a small waterfall stream. We took the chance to get rested and to re-sort our gear, then did some yoga, which was becoming a thing wherever there was a helipad.

After dinner we played cards with another family who'd arrived. Mice nibbled in the night and disturbed my sleep so much that I gave up and left the hut to jump into the river at 5:00 a.m. to have a bracing and reviving icy-cold bath.

The World is Your Pearl

We packed up and headed out after an early breakfast with the full moon still sitting over the mountains to a day which became glorious. With the dappled sun on our backs, we walked through intensely mossy forests of every green imaginable. At one point along the way, we left the packs on the side of the track and walked down to D'Alton Waterfall and Ferguson Falls. Many fungus and lacy, floristically complex mosses covered the ground and carpeted everything, including rocks and fallen logs, creating an oasis of calm throughout the cool, temperate rainforest around us.

At one point along the track, Keron was walking alongside a girl called Brenda. Both had pack covers branded 'Wild Country'. I said, "I've got two wild country girls ahead of me." Keron looked at her and replied, "You can put the girl into the country, but you can't put the country into the girl."

After lots of rock hopping and large tree roots to navigate, we arrived at Windy Ridge Hut at the end of the day, tired and footsore. There was lots of chatter around the dinner table by candlelight, with discussions as to what each of us thought to be the best thing so far about the Overland Track. For Debra, it was 'the top of Cradle Mountain'; for Claire and Keron, 'the view from the 5305 ft summit of Mt Ossa, the highest mountain in Tasmania'; for Emma, 'the people we met along the way'; for me, 'the camaraderie between our group and other people we met; but mostly the millions of magnificent mosses'; for Christine and Katie, 'the whole thing'. We all agreed that so far, this had been a huge personal achievement.

The difficulties of the trek due to weather extremes, and the hardship of having to acquire and carry everything to survive for many days in the wilderness, meant that not many people attempt the Overland, and the like-minded ones who do are those who keep it pristine.

As with all the huts we stayed in, Windy Ridge was another social mecca. Tonight we joined with other trekkers to play Yahtzee. One

From the Cradle to the Lake ~ March 2006 ~

trekker was a man called Dennis. He was down from Queensland's Sunshine Coast where he owned 60 acres in the Glasshouse Mountains and planted native trees. He embraced part of the WWOOF program—*Willing Workers On Organic Farms*—offering cultural exchange employment to backpackers around his property for food and shelter. He also arranged backpacker exchanges to Laughing Waters beef farms in Western Queensland.

As well, he and his family volunteered in third world countries for six weeks at a time 'just doing whatever was needed when they arrived'.

Out here, off the beaten track, it was so refreshing to meet such people who are 'givers' and leave minimal footprints wherever they go.

It had been another big day. We settled for the night to the wafting smells of liniment and heat rubs on cramping legs.

Before breakfast the next morning, on March 17, 2006, we lit candles for Katie's 16th birthday. Each of us had carried small gifts: earrings, chocolate, an anklet, nail polish, a bracelet, and from Katie's mother, Deb, a St Patrick's Day clover with emeralds, on a gold chain. This was a birthday Katie would never forget.

We walked through the magnificent Pine Valley. As Keron and I stopped to drink water, a wombat walked past us. I commented on how very little wildlife there was, and how tiny the bird sounds. There seemed to be very few birds. Keron suggested that maybe the mainland birds were louder because they had to compete with the noise of city and suburban life, whereas the birds here barely have to make a sound in this silent, moss-covered forest.

For miles and silent miles, nothing but a thick cushion of green continued to cover the ground, trees and rocks in electric greens which were accented very occasionally with blood-red or bright-orange fungi. Throughout this wilderness there were a total of 164 species of mosses, 130 liverwort (which made up 60% of Tasmania's bryophytes), and 95 macro lichen species—a truly enchanting fairyland where the closer one looked, the more minuscule detail there was to be seen.

All the girls pushed ahead. Keron and I were having a very hard day, she with leg pain and foot cramps, and me with back pain. To get through it from the beginning, I continued to take six lots of Nurofen a day. Having walked a solid five and a half hours with our heavy packs, we limped into Pine Valley hut at around 2:15 p.m. The rest of the group seemed to be coping pretty well.

We ate, had coffee, walked to a waterfall before dinner, then had chocolates and lit more candles to sing 'Happy Birthday' to Katie. People arrived in the hut from everywhere to join in, one of whom was 'Barry' whose birthday it was as well. He had turned 50. Everyone sang to him too. His speech was, 'he had never had so many people he didn't know to celebrate a birthday'. We all played Gin Rummy by candlelight to lots of conversations and laughter.

Throughout the huts there had been a large number of gastro outbreaks suffered by various people along the way. We were all diligent with hand washing and cleaning the tables well with methylated spirits. We were told about one guy who was travelling with his new partner, hoping to impress her with the trip and all his latest gear. The romance dulled when he came down with severe gastro so badly he had to be airlifted out.

Before bed we hung our food bags from the rafters as mice ran all over the hut at night and licked the plates. Some ran over sleeping people. Best to have cleaned our teeth in case we slept with our mouths open. Nothing was wasted in the bush. Three people had gastro last night. One ran outside to throw up and a possum ate it! Eeew!

From the Cradle to the Lake ~ March 2006 ~

Claire told Dennis his hair looked like shit when we got up in the morning. When we asked him about the possibility of staying at his cabin in the Glasshouse Mountains to do a walk from there, he said, "Yes, of course, but you'll need the address." Claire said, "Your hair looks nice really." Ha ha ha.

Another 'best' thing about this trip was that we were a moving party, with laughter morning to night.

Being a senior nurse at the William Angliss hospital, and a natural leader, we handed Deb the compass and nominated her to lead our seven-hour day trek to the Labyrinth the next morning. Although it was a beautiful climb, the trails were not clear and we needed to stick together. There were lots of specifics for walkers to be aware of up there in the Pine Valley. The dangers were that cloud could move in rapidly and obscure landmarks making track finding difficult.

The weather changes instantly from sun to cloud to rain or snow any time of the year. We were required to take food, water, waterproof clothing, gaiters, sunglasses, jacket and pants, polar fleece, thermals, a thermal or woolen hat and a whistle. Along the way we came across plaques to commemorate one of those who'd perished out there; *Clare Hutcheson 1980-2000. Nature has embraced her forever in this beautiful wilderness;* and another, *Clare, Love and miss you—Chris;* and this, *Clare Hutcheson—aged 20 yrs. Disappeared whilst bushwalking in the area. December 2000. Too young. Too beautiful. Too soon. Mum and Dad. Dec 2001.*

We just couldn't imagine the plight of her demise.

Our beautiful climb up and up to the Labyrinth was blessed with good weather, and although the terrain was tough, the views were spectacular as we ate our lunch at the summit. Dennis also joined us for the climb to the top, and there was lots of laughter as we all

The World is Your Pearl

stood on a huge flat rock, singing 'McArthur Park Is Melting in the Rain' at the tops of our voices; it echoed down the mountainside.

We'd had a ball, but by the time we returned to the Pine Valley Hut, my back and knees had given out. I felt my body was shattered and the painkillers were no longer doing the trick.

Over dinner that night, we had a big conference. Dennis would be moving out at 9:00 a.m. the next morning to take the Lake St Clair ferry from Narcissus Hut at 1:00 p.m. He offered to carry some of my pack weight. Claire and Deb wanted to make the climb to the Acropolis then walk a further 20 kilometres to Echo Point. So we opted to split into two groups and wait two days in Hobart for Deb, Katie, Claire and Christine.

With this decision made, it was a relief to leave the evening's card games and retire.

The hut was abuzz like a beehive. All the strangers we'd met had been excellent. Out here in this peaceful place, everyone is calm and happy to chat, sharing stories and camping tips. The dynamics vary from groups of men in jungle camouflage, to photographers, to families, to solo trekkers.

A new group of men had arrived while we were at the Labyrinth. They were on a scouting reunion and were climbing Marions Peak taking the Eastern slope, when one of their party had a minor stroke. They split up. Two stayed with him, covering him with their sleeping bags.

They were freezing as they waited for hours in the dark while the others went back down Cradle Mountain to the visitors centre to radio for air rescue. The stroke victim had to be stretchered down the mostly vertical mountain, winched out by helicopter and eventually returned to Queensland. The others then completed the Overland

From the Cradle to the Lake ~ March 2006 ~

Track. They were leaving before us. One had a big bushy black beard. He gave us his toilet roll. Claire said, "I could kiss you, but you've got a beard." He said, "That does it, as soon as I get back, I'm going straight to the barbers!" Ha ha ha ha!

It was lovely to lie on the top rack in my sleeping bag, listening to all the hilarity and laughter down below and the screams of elation whenever someone had a win at cards. It was like a little home in the wilderness with a big family. Wet, muddy clothing and socks hung overhead, and a line of soggy boots dried by the wood coal stove. Every day we'd cooked and eaten together, played and laughed together, and when everyone went to bed there were packs and bodies everywhere.

As we settled each night, several minutes of shuffling took place, nestling into sleeping bags, adjusting air mattresses and plumping pillows made of sleeping bag covers stuffed with spare clothes.

That night, the mice and tiny pygmy possums ran rampant over our sleeping bags, rattled in the rubbish bags and over the packs. As one ran over my head, I sat up and lit Claire's head-lamp to shine it into the cabin. Little marsupials ran in every direction. This was their place, after all.

My body was shattered after nine days of traversing up and down very steep mountain slopes with often extreme conditions underfoot. As Keron, Emma, Dennis and I packed up for the last time, the remaining weight of my pack was split three ways with kind offers from Emma and Dennis to carry portions of my gear. Leaving the Pine Valley Hut at 9:00 a.m. we walked out at top speed for our final three-hour walk to Lake St Clair.

After a glass of red wine by an open fire in the Narcissus Hut, I began to unwind. From the terminus we caught the ferry across, and after a bus ride to Hobart and saying our goodbyes to Dennis, we limped into a backpacker's accommodation. I took off my pack and immediately broke down, bursting into tears with my body still in pain, and fatigued. I was strung out, having had to take a lot of painkillers over so many days. We peeled off our reeking boots and clothing and enjoyed steaming hot showers. The feeling of falling into beds with mattresses, sheets, pillows and doonas was divine.

Looking back, I realised that, although I'd done a few training walks with the pack filled with canned food prior to the trek, it hadn't been sufficient. My body had not been ready for such an extremely intense workout. Training is key to the enjoyment of any adventure. Although this had been the biggest physical challenge of my life, I would do it all again in a different way, staying in catered accommodations without the need to carry a full pack.

Apart from the privilege of our immersion into this world heritage wilderness, the huge takeaway for me was the shared life experience I'd had with Emma. As we trekked together as mother and daughter to a place a long way from our comfort zones, while pitting ourselves against so many extremes, it magnified the ever-encompassing love, admiration and respect I had for her abilities and strength of character as a young woman.

CHAPTER 5

How To Sneak Up On Adventure

—Yunnan Province—China ~ 2007 ~

There is a saying
~ 'Never let the truth get in the way of a good story' ~
I'd rather the truth 'be' the good story.

I'm a Capricorn and therefore fairly driven to do and achieve a lot of things, some small, some not so small. One day I was reading an article in a local newspaper about a group of cyclists who'd just returned from an adventure through the back-blocks of ancient Chinese farming villages in the Yunnan Province. They loved it so much they were going back to do it all again. Anyone interested in joining them should ring Dennis Dawson, the leader of the cycling group known as the Warby Ghostriders, on this number …

I'm not sure why, perhaps just because I had nothing to lose and it was the right timing in life with my children no longer living at home, but I picked up the phone and called him. Dennis was a retired physics, science and mathematics teacher with great enthusiasm and zest for an active life, and a real people person.

He'd made a small DVD presentation of the highlights of their trip and said I'd be welcome to come up to Emerald to see it. I went straight away. It looked great. I asked if it was hard. He said anyone with medium physical fitness would have no problem and asked if I'd done much riding. I said, "A bit." But omitted to tell him I'd only made a few attempts, and had all the scars to prove it. However, I booked my place on the 700 kilometre cycling trip, then purchased a bike, then set about learning how to ride.

I was 53 years old and hadn't learned to ride a bike as a child. I was terrified. From the day I took on the challenge, the cold sweats from my terror of riding, fearful of falling and body injuries, stay with me until now. But I was determined to conquer my fears for the long-awaited chance of adventure.

I was taken under the wing of Peter Warren, one of the Ghostriders who became my long-suffering, self-imposed 'coach', and several of the others who took me on as a project. Many, along with their wives, became life-long friends. They encouraged me, tutored me, pushed me when I'd hit the wall, and knew to keep well out of my way. I was a hazard to anyone in my path as I wobbled around, uncoordinated on the bike trails, in danger of clipping their wheels, and, needless to say, I wasn't allowed *near* the roads for a long time. I had eight months to master my cycling skills and get fit.

Having ridden every week for eight months on a heavy mountain bike, I'd come a long way with my cycling fitness. However, I would never have the innate motor skills or confidence of those who had ridden since childhood.

How To Sneak Up On Adventure - China 2007

Riding the Warburton Trail with the Warby Ghostriders

Ready or not, in March, 2007, I was one of fifteen Warby Ghostriders who flew to Kunming.

Along with me were our grand leader, Dennis Dawson, Ken and his son Steven, Viv and Linton, Phil, Jon, Kevin, 'Megga' Mike, Bob, Ross, Noel, Daryl, and Mark. We spent a few days exploring on short rides. Kunming is the capital of the Yunnan Province and is known as the 'City of Eternal Spring' for its pleasant climate and flowers that bloom all year round, and was the gateway to the celebrated Silk Road that facilitated trade with Tibet, Sichuan, Myanmar, India and beyond. It is an ancient route which was used regularly from the time of the Han Dynasty in 130 BCE until the Ottoman closed its routes in 1453 CE.

We visited the Dragon Gate and climbed hundreds of steps high up on Western Mountain and along an extraordinary series of pathways and wormholes cut out of the sheer rock face, which snaked along the ledges of the vertical cliff, where we looked down over the Dianchi Lake 6234 feet below. Sadly we couldn't photograph the lake from our viewpoint as the air was too smoggy.

The paths led through a number of ornately carved, beautifully painted pavilions and garishly decorated grottoes and Buddhist temples of symbolic significance to those who made the pilgrimage to worship. The people were immaculately dressed and well groomed. The main populace wore stylish clothes and many women wore high-heeled shoes, even to climb all the steps up from the Dragon Gate to the top of Western Mountain.

There was a drought in this region of China, and in Kunming they'd had no rain for 47 days. Everything looked parched and dry. The concrete squat toilets on the mountainside were something to behold. I was later to discover that these were some of the better ones in China. Their construction was sturdy, on a concrete base with a simple sloping slot which had to be straddled, and required a good aim. Because there was no water, there was no flushing. 'Oh goody', I was starting to get a feel for *true adventure*.

Back in town, I was confronted as we walked through the markets where cages, so full of beautiful little hummingbirds they could hardly move to flutter their wings, sat out in the blazing sun along with other overcrowded cages of squirrels, mice, terrapins, turtles, rabbits, rodents of all kinds, and boxes of highly coloured baby chicks. It was sad to see a dead one just lifted out and thrown under the counter.

The next day we flew to Li Jiang, about 500 kilometres further to the north-west, to start the big ride. Li Jiang is a town of ancient Chinese architecture in a labyrinth of laneways of rough-hewn cobblestones, worn smooth by human feet and horse hooves. Pretty canals, overhung with willow trees and wisteria, and billowing with roses and cherry blossoms were reflected in the water which teemed with large goldfish.

In the square, the local Naxi people wore traditional costumes of light-blue, loose-sleeved robes, beneath finely pleated black or navy aprons. On their backs were black sheepskins which protected them from the elements when working in the fields. These costumes are symbolic of hard work.

Other minority Chinese women wore colourful, ornate robes. These were complex with heavy embroideries and adorned with fur and silver ornaments. The heavy ornamental headwear was made of beaten silver, and looked spectacular with what appeared to be wrought with a hundred individual flowers standing up on tall stems which shivered above the crowns. The fabrics varied from satin shot with gold, to velvets, brocades and braiding.

Sherpas on horseback wore yak fur vests. Little babies and tiny children were beautifully dressed like little dolls and lovingly cared for, with split pants so they could be held out to squat. Everything was multicoloured and vivid.

This town was joyous with its peaceful, happy people, always smiling. Although there was an incident witnessed by our friend 'Megga' Mike, when he went up to the temple behind the village. As he walked up the hill, a Chinese tour guide had been grabbed by a policeman and was in a headlock with a gun at his head. The gun was waving around while Mike was standing right in front of them.

Mike didn't know which way to jump as a lynch mob of stallholders descended down the hill towards them. He later asked someone what had happened and found out that the tour guide had stabbed and killed a stallholder when he refused to pay him kickbacks he'd demanded. The policeman had been whacking the tour guide at the same time as waving his gun around in an attempt to placate

The World is Your Pearl

the lynch mob. As Mike returned from the temple, he thought the tour guide must have been killed too, as a huge amount of blood was everywhere on the street as though an animal had been slaughtered.

Meanwhile, I was with two other friends, Viv and Linton, shopping. We were having a ball exploring the many shops selling jade, leather handbags, silverware, brass Buddhas, teapots, Tibetan bells, woven shawls and table runners, intricate embroideries and panels from ancient costumes. Silversmiths everywhere were making jewellery and ornaments, engraved bowls and charms.

Our group of 15 Warby Ghostriders were supplied with bikes, and supported all the way by a crew. Our cycling guide was Dave, a bike mechanic we called 'Asia' Mike, (as opposed to our 'Megga' Mike), our interpreter, a lady called Shou Wu, and our back-up vehicle was driven by Glen.

We met up with Dave in the square and went to an amazing upstairs place for dinner. It was built of a creaking labyrinth of wood. A maze of stairways led to little eating nooks. All the walls, floors, tables and chairs were made of smooth old woods which gave off a nutty richness of smell. We ordered an array of various delicious foods. Every dish was a taste sensation of lovely fresh flavours, and *cheap!* We ate and ate and kept ordering more and more dishes and more beer, and the cost only came out at $5 each.

After dinner a lot of us went to the Sakura Cafe for beers. The place was *cranking!* Its ancient timbers were a hive of pits, balconies and alcoves, alive with musicians and a karaoke bar out the back. There were hundreds of people inside and out now, all singing songs in Chinese, and dancing. Young people dressed in traditional costumes sang in large groups 'at' each other across the canal. Each song ended with the call, "Yaso, Yaso, Ya, Ya, Ya". This was the call for the people on the opposite side of the canal to come back with a song. We joined them, coming up with anything from Happy Birthday to the singing slogans from ads for Aeroplane Jelly and Vegemite.

This place went right off at night. It was on for young and old. Everybody was smiling and laughing. We drank a few more beers in the alcoves. I was told the karaoke goes wild later on. If Aussies get up, the crowd plies them with beer and cheers them on for more. Ross was leaving, so I took the chance to go with him as we had an early start to ride in the morning; however, it took ages to get back as there were hundreds of shops to browse until late every night. Ross was looking for a brass Buddha. I was glad he walked back with me as it was late and this *nighttime* Naxi town was a lot quieter, with all the friendly faces gone and replaced with an altogether different dynamic of nightlife characters.

After a cold shower in the morning to the harrowing sounds of pigs screaming and squealing in a nearby abattoir, we geared up and, issued with our bikes for the big ride, tried them out on a 45 kilometre ride out of town through the congested traffic of food markets. Although the roads were muddy, they were flat, and I was pretty pleased with how I navigated through the mayhem of food carts, horses and vehicles. The downside was that it was difficult to breathe as we inhaled the black fumes emitting from diesel trucks, and struggling with the thinner air at an altitude of 7874 feet.

We eventually rode out into rural areas of canola fields where apple blossoms lined the laneways, and over some rough off-road to a place where we had morning tea. Riding further, we visited the beautiful Beiyue Buddhist temple, festooned with prayer flags and fragrant with the smoke of incense.

Back on the bikes, we called into a small remote village of Naxi people. The Naxis are just one of a group of over fifty ethnic minorities in the Yunnan Province. Passing a little school, we all stopped, as Phil, one of our Warby riders, pulled out a plastic frisbee and threw it, creating mayhem. The kids went wild as a few of us had a lot of fun skimming it back and forth into the schoolyard as their teacher looked on, smiling, probably not knowing quite what to make of this alien group in yellow jerseys.

Everywhere we went, there were children and adults running to the roadside calling "Nee How"! "Hello". Dave asked the locals where we could find some amenities. We were pointed to an 'unbelievable' toilet, possibly the only one in town. It was like a wooden crate with one divider, standing on timber slats which had to be navigated across a pit of shit. Jon Bate was on one side. I was on the other. Behind the toilet, large pigs were penned. Their snouts snuffled through an opening where boards were missing at the base of the structure. Obviously there to act as the clean-up crew.

How To Sneak Up On Adventure - China 2007

With the hairs of our nostrils curling and almost scorched from the stench, we were back on the bikes with a decision to opt for 'flower' toilets (finding a bush) wherever possible from then on.

The weather at this time of year was glorious here. Warm balmy days, not too hot, not too cold, with enough rain just to settle the dust. We would halt or slow now and then to pass through cattle or goat herds.

Buffalos pulling ancient ploughs were the only means for farmers to till the earth through these parts of China. Fields everywhere were abundant with wheat, peas and rice. The pace was slow, and we saw no mechanised vehicles, except for the ancient, diesel-powered trucks with their exposed motors. The people had no luxuries to speak of, though it was amusing in any remote place to see satellite dishes or solar power units on rooftops, and labourers in the fields using mobile phones. These were commodities which were dirt cheap to buy in China.

It hadn't taken long to get used to riding on the right side of the road. The traffic here was like slow-motion mayhem, but there was a rhythm which everyone tapped into like the workings of a clock. The people had very little, but their simple way of life seemed to have no stress attached to it.

China is a land of extremes. There had already been a few culture shocks, to say the least, but I was seeing the reality of raw life. The further I went, the more amazing the experiences became.

The World is Your Pearl

Meeting the locals along the way

I was getting a feel for the bike. Each day brought a little more confidence in my handling abilities. For so many months, while learning to ride, I struggled with tight corners and uneven ground. Now I had no choice but to force myself to relax and not grip the handlebars in terror, and, by riding all day every day, it became easier.

We left Li Jiang for another day of riding over a few hills and some good off-road sections to visit Lashi Lake on the southern slope of the Jade Dragon Snow mountain. This was a very watery place. The Lashihai plateau was a wetland nature reserve, a paradise where thousands of migrant birds stay over winter every year. We rode through some tiny Naxi villages along a portion of the Ancient Tea Horse Road. This was once an important trade route in the south-western part of China in ancient times, where the horse was the significant form of transport.

There was plenty of rural life. The people stared and some waved as we meandered past. Their daily existence is based on farming around poetically named water sources such as 'The Beauty Spring', 'Holy Well Source' and 'Seven Fairies Lake'.

They are all fed from the melting snow of the Jade Dragon Snow Mountain. The road is more like a trail with nothing but the occasional horse or bullock. It is quiet and peaceful, and everything is lush, green and beautiful with fragrant blossoms on fruit trees in orchards along the roadsides.

After a lovely three hours of riding, a picnic lunch of buns, cold meats, salads, fruit, nuts and a form of sweet biscuit with tea and coffee appeared from nowhere and was laid out ready on trestle tables as we arrived in a lush orchard beside the beautiful Zhi Yun Buddhist Monastery.

The monks allowed us to take photos inside where thousands of metres of vividly colourful Chinese silks and satins hung from the rafters of the temple. They were stitched in the shapes of overlapping men's neckties in separate colours of red, yellow, orange, blue, green and purple. The opulence was difficult to take in. Beneath the enormous golden Buddhas sat huge offerings bowls filled with pearls. Ornate brass urns, inlaid with intricate cloisonné, enamel designs were filled with flowers. Exquisite tapestries hung along walls, between glass cabinets of prayer books nestled in handmade fabric cases. On pedestals sat lovingly tended ancient bonsai trees of pine and spruce. I felt privileged to be able to see such a hallowed place as we padded through in our socked feet.

We rode on for the afternoon, and returned to Li Jiang for dinner at the Sakura Cafe again. In the evening I did a spot of shopping, and purchased some polar fleece clothing and a Gortex jacket before starting the big ride in the morning.

The World is Your Pearl

The BIG ride turned out to be a 'mountainous' six hundred kilometres, which Dennis jokingly called 'undulating'! Now the challenge really began.

Riding the back roads out of Li Jiang we stopped at Baisha Village where some local musicians practised. As we stopped to listen, they shyly beckoned us over. I sat in with them and tried my hand at playing one of their stringed instruments made of wood and snake skin. Their music was so jangly and discordant I couldn't relate to any of the sounds and was beside myself with laughter, much to their bewilderment.

Musicians, Baisha Village. Photo - Phil Jones

It was only 40 kilometres but the riding was tough as we rode up and up through pine forests and the snow-capped peaks of Jade Dragon Snow Mountain. We descended into Bai Shui He, where majestic yaks stood in calcified water terraces, formed as a result of the heavy mineral-laden mountain waters reacting to sunlight.

At an altitude of 7808 feet, the area was very cold. Our accommodation for the night was like a ski chalet. Somehow, my single room accommodation was not available and I was asked to share with Viv and Linton due to a last-minute mix-up. Our room was well appointed, though unheated. However there *were* electric blankets on the beds. I'd only had one hot shower since arriving in China, and tonight's was to be another cold one.

At dinner, we almost froze as we ate in an unheated building. We could see the breath vapours coming from our mouths, although conversations remained animated throughout the group. The subject of my 'mixed' sleeping arrangements with Viv and Linton came up. It was discovered that in China, this practice was very much against Chinese custom. Linton brought the house down as he acted out a dramatic, full-bodied, hip-thrusting, forwards-and-backwards 'in-out' motion, with a very theatrical face, suggesting he'd be right for the night. Everyone roared with laughter.

I was glad of all the pre-training I'd done to get my bike fitness, as the next day was over 78 kilometres of hard riding. The first of two ascents took us over a smooth paved road up into the mountains through some of the most spectacular scenery of the trip. A speedy downhill followed, with lots of hairpin bends, and brought us to the second big climb up a cobblestoned road to a height of 10,712 feet.

I was dreading the next stretch which was a 38 kilometre downhill ride over rough cobblestones.

Apart from Dave, who never let me out of his sight, everyone had ridden ahead but Jon Bate, a racing car driver and fellow cyclist. I called him GJ, 'Gentleman Jon'. He was gracious and kind-hearted. He stayed back, watching me. Before he took off he gave me a tip.

The World is Your Pearl

"Get your backside off the seat just a couple of centimetres. Keep your hands loose and just let the bike do the work." Then he was gone, and I was left on the mountain-top with the wind whistling through my helmet.

Fortunately the Capricorn Mountain Goat in me found the nerve to launch off the top and traverse down the mountain. It was at this point that Jon's advice gave me a whole new approach to trusting myself, and the bike and its suspension, letting the bike go over the loose stuff. I was in a cold sweat with fear as I navigated big potholes or jutting cobblestones. Some areas were very steep, and there were a few sharp corners to creep around while dreading another vehicle coming towards me. In just over three hours there was distant clapping and cheering from the riders waiting at the bottom. This was a highlight for me and I was encouraged by everyone's enthusiasm and elated with a newfound confidence in my riding ability.

We rode on to our lunch spot further down the mountain in Daju where Phil brought out his second frisbee to the delight of some children in the laneway. We were shown into the little Snowflake Cafe where, seated on tiny plastic stools, we ate a glorious multifaceted lunch. Bowl after bowl of delicious local produce of fresh peas, broccoli, mushrooms, greens, tomatoes and rice appeared.

After more fun in the lane with the children, we rode out to the edge of a steep cliff about a kilometre above the Yangtze River. A group of local porters carried our bikes down to a barge, to be taken across the river and back up for another eight kilometres to waiting trucks who transported us and our bikes on to the town of Haba.

It was on these cliff edges where I rediscovered my phobia of heights. Two of our Warby friends, Ken and his son Steven, 'fed' me down the cliff face to the barge. The ledges up the other side were even worse. Another friend Noel assisted further, balancing on the absolute outer edge to shield me from seeing the sheer drop below. I was distressed and paranoid. One slip and he'd be gone. Eventually, after much protestation from me, he went behind, with Dave in front, talking me through all the way.

With a lot of tag-teaming between Jon holding one hand and Dave the other, we eventually came out on a more open trail. I flew up from there, until reaching yet another ledge on a precipice, where vertigo-round-two kicked in. I was in awe of the porters who sprinted along these ledges with the bikes over their shoulders. Once at the top, the bikes were loaded into a large truck, and 4WDs took us to Haba. The drive was unbelievable. Passing a small village on the plateau, one remote house had a huge dog in a small cage, kept like a rabbit ready to eat. The climb and descent were glorious across vast heights, the scale of this landscape cannot be described. It was so high and so deep it couldn't be captured on camera.

The Haba guesthouse where we were to stay was a wooden premises on the edge of another cliff, with small, spartan rooms. Like everywhere in China, the beds were hard but surprisingly comfortable, I guess because I was so tired at the end of a day's riding it was great to lay down the weary bones.

The guesthouse was run by a very energetic lady called Shou Li. She was always smiling, and moved at a run. All we wanted when we arrived was a hot shower. However, surprise, surprise, another coldy.

The 'shower' was a free-standing room like a container, across from the main building, and had a tank stand at the side with a supposed hot water service above. Shou Li walked across, carrying a thermos of hot water for Viv.

The World is Your Pearl

Viv and Linton were both inside. Linton is a big, tall, handsome redhead. Shou Li stuck her head in like a chicken with its head through the wire, and froze in shock at the sight of the two naked bodies, then came running back, screaming with embarrassed laughter, with her hands over her mouth. It's illegal for men and women to shower together in China, even if married. Little did she know they weren't, and that only the night before he'd slept in the same room with 'two' women!

Dinner was another enormous affair as we all huddled around two low tables covered with contact adhesive in a smoky room where Shou Li cooked for twenty of us (including our crew). In two huge woks above a wood-fuelled fire, she produced ten to twelve delicious dishes per table.

The next morning she served banana pancakes followed by eggs and tomatoes with coffee to finish. Shou Li's family ate quite a different breakfast of dough dumplings with chilli, pickled radish and pickled cabbage, followed by yak butter tea. Shou Li churned the yak butter while sitting by the fire where the tea was steeping. Once combined, it looked like a curdled mess. None of us were game to try it, though we were told by the locals that it was delicious.

Shou Li's Pickled Radish Recipe:
Radish, very cold water, ginger, garlic, salt, sugar.
In jar—Six days—Eat.

For the small fee of 25 yuan (AUD$4) each, she offered to take a group of us up the mountain to visit her village. Six of us wanted to go, and, as we stepped out, there were a couple of travellers from Arizona, setting out on a two-day climb up to the peak beyond where we were headed. They had four huge packs which were loaded onto a little donkey and we all set out for a short way together. As we branched off we climbed and climbed, seemingly in the middle of nowhere; following a stream of loose stones we passed a little mosque on the side of the mountain.

How To Sneak Up On Adventure - China 2007

Families laboured together in their tiered fields. Two little children in tattered clothes and old sand shoes played at carrying a small iron bar balanced between two sticks. They were having so much fun, laughing and giggling, as happy as could be.

Shou Li was like a mountain goat. She offered to take my day pack but I declined, I didn't need it carried, though Kevin took it instead. From the pocket of her apron we were given old crinkled apples for morning tea, and preserved ginger for prevention of altitude sickness.

In a tiny village at the top, we were invited inside the home of one of the Yi families. A simple slab hut with an open pit fire in the centre surrounded by tiny wooden stools and other small pews (probably borrowed from neighbouring villagers for the occasion of our visit). Cardboard and sheets of raffia were slung

Chatting to a local Village Yi Lady near Haba, Yunnan Province

up, serving as wall dividers in three corners with a small bed in each. In the fourth corner was an old armchair near a store of potatoes. They barely had anything, except for a big TV and a satellite dish outside!

The Yi women wore large black head pieces, like flattened box kites, signifying that they had children. The young girls wore small embroidered bonnets. When a daughter had children the mother presented her with a large headpiece. The older ladies wore little caps.

We took three hours to climb up and one hour to come down, fortunately via a different route which seemed shorter, easier and less technical. By the time we returned to the guesthouse I felt really ill, possibly from a combination of sun stroke, altitude sickness and dehydration, as Kev had been carrying my water supply and was often way above me or sometimes behind me as we'd climbed. While the others enjoyed lunch I went to lie down in my room. I had the shivers, and felt no better as everyone started to gear up to get back on the bikes.

I had to opt for the 'sag wagon' and travel with Shou Wu in the support vehicle, along with another of our group, Mark, who was suffering from gastro. I was wishing the whole way that I could be riding, as this section was a seven kilometre descent over smooth bitumen, though as hairy as Mickey Mouse and Donald Duck going around the Grand Canyon, with sheer drops of hundreds of feet to the Yangtze River below. The van pulled up now and then to stay back as the riders went ahead. I got out and took a couple of photos, wishing madly that I could be on the ride.

As the saying goes, 'Be careful what you wish for'. About 12 kilometres from the end of our day's journey, the van pulled up again. Daryl had crashed badly doing 75kph on a hairpin bend. There was blood everywhere. He had a bleeding nose, and skin off his knee and hand. Worse off was his chin, which was deeply lacerated, requiring stitches, and his shoulders which took the brunt of the fall, subsequently necessitating two years of operations as a result.

In order to make room for Daryl to travel in the van, I was required to vacate my seat and don the helmet to ride the final 12 kilometres through the Tiger Leaping Gorge. This was a bad move. I discovered I was really not well at all, and, once again, GJ came to the rescue. Jon 'pushed' me with his hand on my back for nine kilometres. I couldn't believe his strength. I kept wanting to get off and walk, but he kept pushing. I couldn't even hold my arm up for that long, much less push someone uphill against what was becoming a strong headwind.

The rocky overhangs had to be seen to be believed. I couldn't imagine how the road builders had the engineering skills to create these roads, much less how the whole lot didn't come crashing down on them. Travelling in the gorge did pose some risks. There were often landslides. While the trips were scheduled outside the landslide season, their occurrence was not something the team operators could judge, and safety couldn't always be guaranteed. We had to sign a waiver when we booked the trip to say we'd take that risk.

I was so relieved when we finally limped into Sean's Walnut Garden Guesthouse.

This was an utterly incredible inn on a precipice. Sean, the owner, had been there for 24 years and had created something quite amazing. It was a mecca for travellers from all over the world and had a real vibe and feel to it.

Slabs of stone formed tables, and comfy slatted wooden chairs were scattered everywhere amongst pot plants, bonsais and little gnarled walnut trees which grew out of the ledges. Everything was well appointed with ensuites to every room. Nice varnished rock walls on the interior, carpet on the floors, TV, hot and cold water, and a kettle to make tea in my room. The girls worked very hard serving food 'all day' and doing any washing required. Safety is 'zero'. Everything balanced on the brink. Balustrades were rickety, electrical wiring ran everywhere, and the large stones in the steps were loose. But the scenery was breathtaking.

The view before us was of two kilometres of vertical rock face soaring from the sky above us, down to the Yangtze River deep in the canyon below. The power and immensity of this couldn't be seen in one look without craning to look up, up, up or, (for me, trying not to look) down, down, down.

Some of the others went off on a four-hour hike up the mountain behind us. I was glad to chill out for a while catching up with my journal writing. Daryl was very sore and sorry. Mark's gastro came good, but Linton spent the day suffering from it. We all retreated in our own ways. I was still feeling ill, and shattered with fatigue, and went to bed early.

The next morning the others said they'd never laughed so much in their lives as they had last night. There was marijuana in everything they ate. The menu offered 'happy smoke', 'happy pancake', happy anything. Mark had a happy pancake for breakfast, and we didn't see him for the rest of the day! It was probably in everything because, although I didn't specifically order any 'happy' meals, I was super chilled and just did some sketches and basked in the sun for the rest of the day.

Everyone was relaxed and this free day was much needed in every respect as we knew tomorrow and the next day would be dangerous and hard.

How To Sneak Up On Adventure - China 2007

The following morning began with banana porridge under the 'big top', an enormous fancy awning which Sean had erected the previous night for everyone to have their dinner beneath. We departed in high spirits right on time. I felt fit and well again, Linton and Mark were over their gastro, but Daryl had to travel in the van because of his injuries. It was a long day of cycling for 75 kilometres, travelling over some hairy terrain out of the gorge.

The depth of the gorge is an astonishing 13,123 feet. Four kilometres of sheer vertical rock face straight up from the Yangtze River to the highest point. This utter scale made it virtually impossible to photograph. We rode through waterfalls, over avalanches and landslides across the road. The road itself was coming away in parts and was simply patched up with a bit of tar. Two men stood about 400 ft up, on a ledge; they were jack-hammering! On the road beneath them were star picket posts and chicken wire, supposedly to shield passersby against falling rocks from above.

We had to ride up and down some really rough rocky rubble with no barricades on the outside. With a sheer drop three kilometres down to the Yangtze, I held my breath as we passed occasional oncoming diesel trucks and buses.

After a two-hour struggle, it was like being set free to come out onto smooth bitumen again, to ride fast downhill around another multitude of hairpin bends. We stopped at a spot almost out of the gorge for morning tea, then continued downwards along the Yangtze, eventually crossing it over a bridge.

Our ride 'undulated' back along the other side until lunchtime. It was astounding to look upwards to where we'd ridden the road kilometres above us. The sense of freedom was beautiful. We just rode to eat. Being fed delicious fresh food three times a day without a care in the world, with nothing to do but enjoy the challenge and each other's company. Strong lifetime bonds were established as

The World is Your Pearl

Sketch of the road through Tiger Leaping Gorge

we synced together, sharing the privilege of participating in an extraordinarily unique experience which not many people on earth would get to have.

The food everywhere was delicious. Lunch in the little cafe by the river consisted of fried rice, fresh broad beans, greens, chilli and a delightful 'mint' tea. Further on we crossed another bridge, back over the Yangtze, and rode on for another two hours to the afternoon tea spot. Phil bought me an ice cream. As I wandered around eating it I came across a really sad-looking dog on a short chain. Thinking I was about to pat it, David and 'Megga' Mike yelled out "DON'T"!

How To Sneak Up On Adventure - China 2007

Rabies is rampant throughout China and it can be deadly. The treatment for someone infected is a long and horrible ordeal of many injections over several months.

Chickens were sitting, four to a tiny cage, unable to move around, with no water to drink. All the dogs were underfed, bone thin, mangy and filthy, tethered on short ropes or chains or in small cages, often without a water bowl.

The fields right through China are lush and abundant with every imaginable crop of grains and vegetables. Throughout the valley we passed miles of strawberry fields. Their flavour was rich, sweet and luscious. The tomatoes, peas and broad beans too were incredibly flavoursome. In fact all the produce had an intense richness of full, natural flavour I hadn't tasted before. The Yangtze was very majestic. We stopped at a spot where the current ran down one side and up the other. Small paddle boats with little outboard motors could be hired to traverse the circuit which ran around a huge sand bank.

At the end of the day we arrived in Shigu. It was abuzz with flies. The roadside food appeared to be grey slabs of tripe. A woman walked past us wearing a frilly white, wide-brimmed hat. Across her shoulders balanced a yoke with two steaming buckets of shit. Possibly off to feed the pigs or fertilise a crop? Another ancient lady, with a weathered face like a polished walnut, smiled as she walked towards us in the street. She was carrying a muddy duck, which she placed upside down on her head.

There was rubbish everywhere. The area we stayed in stank of animal and human excrement, and the rooms reeked of stale cigarette smoke. I had a lukewarm shower to wash off the day's grit and diesel fume grease which permeated my skin. Ross and I wandered around the town, looking at some grimy shops, where I bought three strings of tiny Tibetan bells.

The World is Your Pearl

A local Shigu lady with her duck

When we returned, a huge bowl full of freshly picked strawberries was being rinsed in 'local' water. This concerned me. The trip was run through a Chinese company who didn't insist on using bottled water, and I wondered if we would become ill. The strawberries were a treat for us. Our crew had sent Shou Wu back to purchase them from a roadside stall next to the strawberry fields where they grew. I have never tasted such full-flavoured strawberries before or since. Amazingly and thankfully none of us got sick.

There was a children's 100-day party going on in the courtyard of our accommodations. In China, it is traditionally believed that the first 100 days after the child's birth is the most vulnerable period for both the mother and the newborn; therefore, they are advised to stay home to avoid contracting diseases. This is why making it through the first 100 days is the perfect time to celebrate. The place was bedlam with the kids screaming and yelling out of control,

How To Sneak Up On Adventure - China 2007

as they scrambled around the food table. The food consisted of a large dish of pigs lungs, another of ducks tongues, fatty pork, offal, and various dishes I didn't recognise, all oozing with flies. An enormous cauldron of steamed rice was carried in from up the street. We watched as some potato chips were washed under a roadside pipe. Some which fell into the gutter were gathered up and placed back in with the others. Our food started to be delivered. I opted out and went up to my room for a cup of my own sachet coffee and a bag of lollies for dinner. Bad luck about the carbs I'd need for the 90-kilometre ride uphill tomorrow, but I wouldn't be eating breakfast here either!

Darling David knocked on my door to ask if he could get me some food from somewhere else. When I said I didn't need anything, he went down and brought back bananas, apples and oranges. He was such a 'spoiler'. I must have been feeling strung out, as the racket here seemed huge. My nerves were on edge with dogs barking, people yelling and talking non-stop, as loud trucks rattled down the cobblestoned road beside us. I couldn't wait to leave here. I walked down to see if I could visit the statue of Chairman Mao, but the roads were unlit and it was too dark to see.

Everyone chipped in 20 yuan ($2.50) as Dennis had organised a box of giant fireworks for our evening's entertainment. These included sky rockets and various explosives. We all walked to the park to let them off. People came from everywhere. I was asked to hold on to a rocket launcher. I didn't want one, but everyone had one, so Glen lit mine and ash fell down everywhere as it repeatedly let out fuses which exploded high into the sky.

Next were the ground-based fireworks. BIG mothers! As big as a person's leg. One fell over and sent explosives in all directions. We all ran around in circles bumping into each other. One went through Kevin's legs as another whizzed past Ross's earhole. I've never laughed so hard in the face of danger. I turned to run off and ran into 'Megga' Mike, who fell down on the ground in fits of laughter. Police sirens went off as we scattered home, still aching with laughter.

Back in the courtyard of our accommodation, we stood in a circle, recapping the 'incident' and marvelling at how Dave, as our tour leader, could have allowed such an activity. It could have potentially been disastrous. Dave joked about ringing the owner of the tour company and saying, "Er, we lost seven people out of our tour." "No, it wasn't a bike crash." "No, they didn't go over the gorge." "Er, um." He was hilarious. The night had turned out a 'cracker' in every respect.

Breakfast was a bowl of clear soup with tomatoes and noodles. I ate some. Not a lot of nourishment for the big ride we had ahead.

It's always a real buzz setting out together in the mornings. Today would be our longest ride of 91 kilometres with a number of long, up-hill stretches. I had to get off and walk with the bike a fair bit as the cadence was such that I'd slowed down to 6 kph. I can 'walk' uphill at 5 kph.

Because I had no bike skills from an early age, the slow grind uphill, without the ability to ride 'off the seat' was agony. David rode along beside me while I pedalled slowly. We chatted comfortably for around 17 kilometres. He told me his dad had died when he was nine years old. He'd had a pretty tough life, though with his sparkling Pommy sense of humour, you'd never know it.

We met up with the others for morning tea. Shou Wu gave a skinny tethered dog some biscuits. We fed him bits of boiled egg and apple cores, and filled his water dish. Back on the bikes we rode past tar pits, then stone and concrete works where the air was choked with dust. Workers carved statues and monuments with electric drills and saws, with no face masks or ear protection in sight. It started to rain, and filthy, black road muck was splashed up onto my yellow jersey.

The ride was flat into the town where we stopped for lunch. Everything seemed miniature in China. Wherever we ate, we were seated on tiny plastic stools. Linton and 'Megga' Mike struggled with them.

Except for our experience in Shigu, the food throughout China was always appetising and delicious. Outside the cafe, I took photographs of a monstrous tangle of electrical wiring suspended from a corner lamp post. This seemed to be standard everywhere in rural China.

On a bedlam ride out of town, I was feeling pretty pleased with myself, controlling the bike as I wound slowly between so much chaotic traffic. Out into the country again the road was undulating and beautiful. I got my second wind as I flew uphill, passing everyone.

Three hours later, heading towards Shaxi, Dennis came off his bike, skinning his nose and chin. Jon Bate was taken down with him as they were both squeezed off the road by heavy traffic and their handlebars locked. They had nowhere to go. Dennis looked really funny, like Brutus out of Popeye the Sailor Man, with half the dirt of China on his chin. They sported some bruises for a few days.

It was around 5:30 p.m. when we arrived in Shaxi where we stayed in the beautiful Tea & Horse Caravan Inn. It had enclosed courtyards with gardens billowing with vegetables, peony roses and bonsai plants. I was given a bed in the upstairs store room where bags of grain and clay pots of pickled things fermented, and pigs' legs hung suspended from the rafters. Viv and Linton were given another tiny store room at the top of a very steep staircase. All the windows were shuttered and ornate.

The World is Your Pearl

As there was no hot running water, a dish and thermos of hot water from a kettle was brought to each room. On the main veranda, we ate dinner together, served by our gracious and dignified hosts.

We stayed for two nights. I enjoyed the time catching up on washing, journal writing and going out shopping, where I bought a pair of 'Warby' yellow runners which matched our Warby Ghostriders jerseys.

The town was lovely with a river which ran behind it next to farmland.

At some time in the afternoon, as the group sat around together going over our photos of the trip so far, one friend took my camera and offered to condense my images in order to create more space on the camera card. This ended badly. Somehow he accidentally erased all the photos of my trip. I couldn't believe they were suddenly lost forever. He felt terrible. His heart had been in the right place, and no way did he mean for this to happen, but I was utterly devastated.

I tried to console myself by thinking, in ten years from now, will it really matter? Telling myself this was most definitely a 'first-world' problem. In comparison to the poverty of the places we'd ridden, seeing the hard lives of the Chinese, I needed to get over it. But no matter how I tried to deal with it, it was a hard call. I was awake at 2:00 a.m., stewing with disappointment, thinking of all the lovely shots I'd lost of the weathered faces of the Yi and Naxi people, the heart-stopping drama of the Tiger Leaping Gorge, the ancient architecture throughout the Yunnan Province, all the memories and moments in time.

I listened to the clock downstairs chime 2:30, 3:00, 3:30, 4:00, 4:30, 5:00 a.m., then got up and went down for a 'cold' shower and got dressed, ready to ride.

How To Sneak Up On Adventure - China 2007

Today was to be a diabolically steep ride uphill over large cobblestones, followed by a rough dirt off-road downhill. It would be a distance of 38 kilometres in total, until lunchtime. The weather had turned and it was raining heavily.

David took us to a coffee house for a heart starter, on him, before setting out. He was unusually quiet. I had to ask him to tell me what was wrong. He told me that the day before he'd had some bad news from back home in England. His gran had died. He was so upset. The spark had gone from him, and me, for different reasons.

Though ready in my rain gear, I decided I wasn't physically able to ride 'up' on the rough. Accepting my limitations, I opted to travel in the sag wagon with Daryl and Shou Wu. By now it was pouring with heavy, soaking rain along very dangerous, slippery roads all the way.

Local vendors were huddled on the sides of the road under umbrellas, trying to sell their wares. They looked cold, wet and miserable. We passed a herd of buffalo as their herdsman sat huddled next to the little wood fire he'd built.

We arrived at the lunch spot cafe around 11:30 a.m. It was freezing as we sat around a tiny brazier trying to keep warm. At 12:30 p.m 'Megga' Mike sent a radio message through to Glen, our support driver, to say that he and the other riders were still 20 kilometres away. By 1:30 p.m. there was still no sign of them. I was thinking their ride must have been a shocker. Kevin had had a cold for five days and it had turned into the flu. He would be doing it really hard.

Shou Wu made a warming ginger tea, sweetened with palm sugar. We waited a further three hours as the rain continued to pour. At last I heard someone's voice say, "Ahh". I Looked up and there they all came, covered in blood. There must have been a severe accident. Another look made me realise it was not blood, but

The World is Your Pearl

dark-red clay mud. The riders and bikes were caked from head to toe. Their shoes, pedals and tyres were so thick with mud they could only slip along in some places. The mud had filled the tread of the tyres and gathered up stones which then got caught as they went around, sending the bikes into skids.

A friendly farmer had invited them all into his home for a hot cup of tea and a rest. The local school children came out of their classrooms to gape and laugh at what may have been the first Western people they'd ever seen, and mad, crazy at that—all on bikes, covered in mud, wearing helmets and yellow Warby jerseys.

As the riders trailed into our lunch place, the linoleum floor was red mud from one end to the other.

All the guys, and Viv, were abuzz, describing the whole ordeal. Bob was not happy. He was livid that they had been subjected to the difficulties of that section of the journey, saying, "If someone had been injured, it would have been a helicopter job." (Though I'd never seen a chopper or a light aircraft in any of the places we'd been in China.) The condition of that normally dry, dusty area had been turned to mud, due to unexpected, torrential rain.

As we ate our lunch, people said, "Wise move, Glenda Wise, you would have hated every minute of that ride." Viv told me I would have been in tears trying to get through the sticky mud for 38 kilometres. We had driven 62 kilometres to meet them at the lunch place. The trail they'd ridden was not accessible by vehicle. I don't think any wheels were meant to go where they went.

They had cleaned a lot of the mud from the bikes with water from a flowing concrete canal next to a village at the bottom of the descent. Some dunked their bikes in it. They found out later it was the town's water supply.

After lunch, I got back on the bike and continued with the others to ride the remaining 23 kilometres to Er Yuen.

After a hellish day, our accommodation in Er Yuen was very palatial with two natural hot-spring-fed pools. The rooms were heated and luxurious. We just dropped our bags, had hot showers, got into our bathers and jumped in.

Outside in the cold and rain, Dave, Shou Wu, 'Asia' Mike and Glen worked for hours cleaning the mud off the bikes with toothbrushes. We went across the road for a dinner of 20 shared dishes, with more dishes continuing to come. Dave looked spent. He still had to go back and check all the bikes' brakes and their mechanical soundness for tomorrow's ride.

When I returned to the hotel, I bumped into Ken and Steven. Steve asked me to give him my corrupted SD camera card to take back to Australia to attempt to recover some of my images. He exchanged it with the memory card from his PDA (Personal Diary Assistant). It had held his favourite music, downloaded from home before the trip to listen to on the ride. He deleted it all, and reformatted it to give me half a gig of photo space. It was such an incredible kindness from a young man. Ken must have been proud of him. I was so grateful as we were very remote and far from shops which sold tech stuff. Once back in Australia, I was thrilled that Steve had somehow been able to recover half of the images I'd lost.

Back in my room, I got back into my wet bathers and went out for another plunge into the hot spring pool to swim a few laps. The weather was freezing cold and raining. As I returned to my room, I could see Dave, Shou Wu, Glen and 'Asia' Mike still working on the bikes in the dark for several more hours.

It rained all night and in the morning before breakfast we were packed, showered and ready to leave at 9:00 a.m. There had been so many problems with the bikes, caused by the jamming of mud and stones, that departure was delayed until 10:30 a.m.

This gave me another chance to get into my bathers and back into the spring water pool which was even hotter this morning.

Today's itinerary read:

> ... *We follow a circuitous route that takes us to Er Hai Lake. We skirt the shores of this huge inland sea, passing through fishing villages and farming communities before taking a ferry ride across to the other side. This is a spectacular finale as we head up the hill towards the ancient walled capital of Dali. The Cangshan Mountains rise behind Dali as we cycle our last few kilometres to our finishing point.*

Today would be our 13th day. When the bikes were fixed, we finally rode out together, past a whole cow being butchered on the roadside. Cycling on, we shared the road with bell-laden horses and carts as we continued to travel on the Old Tibet Road to Dali.

I had been amazed by the hard physical labour in rural China. I saw no tractors or mechanised equipment, and all the back-breaking work was done manually, with the aid of beasts of burden and handmade implements.

People gathered and shovelled animal and human manure to put back into the soil. Every piece was collected into buckets, physically carried on yokes across shoulders, tipped into carts pulled by oxen, horses or bullocks to deposit in neat piles along the roadsides of farms. Each pile was gathered again into buckets and distributed into the fields.

Thousands of crops stretched as far as the eye could see in any direction, all dotted with little bent-back people in coolie hats, working the rich earth.

Even little children worked alongside their parents. Babies and toddlers were worn in slings on their parents' backs while seeds were sown. The harvests were abundant. Everything was picked, gathered and stacked mountainous on people's backs, or onto carts pulled by donkeys. Some carts or trailers were mobilised by the human pedal-power of rusty pushbikes. They peddled and shifted and moved and carried from daylight till dark.

Although I mostly trailed far behind the others, I minced and ground my way up and up the roads through the Yunnan Province where the air was often thin, making it difficult to breathe at altitude in elevations which varied from the mountain peaks to river valleys by as much as 9800 feet.

We'd ridden down over the Yangtze River and on through the Tiger Leaping Gorge.

The World is Your Pearl

Throughout the mountains, the roads were continually destroyed due to earthquakes, tremors, landslides, water and rock falls which caused huge death rates of many commuters and road builders. Several times we had to carry our bikes over the rubble of rock slides, or pick our way underneath waterfalls carrying the bikes.

There were no road barriers except for the occasional concrete block at various intervals as we rode for days. We were dwarfed like ants by walls of vertical rock, around roads cut out of the vast mountain with a sheer drop of thousands of feet to the Yangtze River below. It was both exhilarating and nail-biting stuff, and the start of many such adventures.

This trip had been immense, both physically and emotionally. Our group of Warby Ghostriders became strongly bonded as lifelong friends. We would travel many thousands of kilometres together through other regions of the earth in the years to come.

I was hooked so much that I returned to China the following year for a 700-kilometre ride along the limestone trail of the Karst Mountains from Guiyang to Yangshuo.

CHAPTER 6

Don't Pat the Yaks— Nepal ~ 2009 ~

Walking is an athletic endeavour to be done poorly or well. The Nepalese do it supremely well
—Jack Bennett, The Art of Walking.

The Warby Ghostriders cycling group I rode with were a large number of acquaintances who gathered in various-sized pelotons to cycle each week. Several of us began to embrace more and more forms of adventure travel. This time, as a change from cycling, it was to be a trek on foot through Nepal.

The majority of us lived locally to each other within Victoria. Along with our leader, Dennis Dawson, was myself, Gael, Mike, Monika, Viv, Linton, Kev, Linda, Karen, Paul, Barb, Noel and Rick. The preparations, down to every detail, were arranged by World Expeditions, the company I have continued to travel with until the present day.

The World is Your Pearl

We flew to Kathmandu, where we stayed for two nights and got a taste of a city steeped in religion. Dominating its centre, and fluttering with thousands of prayer flags, stood the largest stupa in Nepal. This was the vast and imposing whitewashed Boudhanath. Built in the 14th century, it was one of the most sacred sites in Tibetan Buddhism outside of Tibet. Its ancient brass prayer wheels were turned constantly by worshippers and a large congregation of Buddhist monks in red and saffron robes.

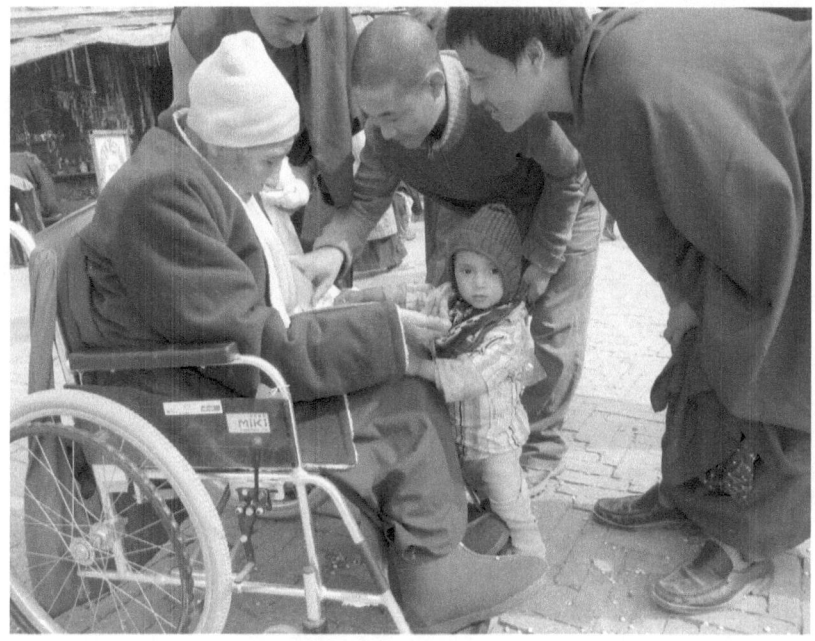

At Boudhanath Stupa, Kathmandu

I watched a small group of monks lovingly attending to an old lama as he was taken along in his wheelchair. They stopped in the middle of the square and a tiny child went across to see him as he fed some pigeons from a dish of corn. The lama feebly touched the little child on the head and shared his corn for him to feed the pigeons too. It was a tender moment.

Don't Pat the Yaks—Nepal ~ 2009 ~

Elsewhere was the Pasupatinath, a Hindu temple by a grey river, floating with scum and rubbish. This was a sacred place where a cremation was taking place. Professional holy men painted in ash posed in their robes for photos. We were driven mad by persistent hawkers who swarmed all over us, pressing their wares of jewellery, brass ornaments and coloured powders.

On a hill overlooking Kathmandu, the skies darkened as we climbed the many steps to visit the Monkey Temple in the forest. It was another beautiful stupa where we entered to listen to the sounds of deep resonant drums and conch shells while 40 monks chanted mantras. Its colourful interior was fragrant with burning incense, and glowed with golden light from candles and lamps. Monkeys roamed around outside as a large electrical storm shattered the silence.

The following day we were issued with distinctive red bags which would be used by the porters to carry our essentials for the trek. Once packed, the rest of our gear was stored at the hotel until our return.

We flew to Pokhara where we were taken by bus on an hour's journey to the village of Khere. It began to rain as we set out from here on foot.

Donning wet weather gear, we trekked for five hours, along a trail which wound uphill through terraced fields and mixed oak and rhododendron forests. A camp was established where we would sleep in tents for the first night on a grassy ridge known as Australia Camp. I took a walk with a few of the girls to a clearing further up, where we sat to meditate at dusk. The lights of Pokhara could be seen, twinkling in the distance over a thousand feet below.

As I began the trek on day one, en route to Annapurna, I thought I was going to die. Being used as I was to a fast-paced life of anything from running, to a brisk walk to do things, I was suddenly

The World is Your Pearl

faced with having to stay behind the mountain guide at a pace so painfully slow that my mind was screaming, "Let me past."

One step, two steps, three steps in slow motion. This was how it was to be for two weeks over often vertical mountain slopes.

There is a wonderful book called *Travelers' Tales Nepal: True Stories of life on the Road* by Rajendra S. Khadka. One of the tales was by Jack Bennett, who described the Nepalese art of walking:

> ~ ... *As each day passed, our group of trekkers mirrored his rhythm. My mind and entire being began to slow, and I fell into a calm timelessness. I had nothing to do but to enjoy the view. I had learned a different way to walk. With the upper body quiet and balanced, the work was in the legs. In no time it was easy to acquire a graceful, efficient and mindful walking style which became even more effortless as I slowed my pace by taking smaller steps.*
>
> *I watched the Nepalis and I noticed that they take such small steps that they walk almost toe to heel. As I followed their rhythm I found small steps uphill to be less tiring, though taking more, the cumulative effect was less. Small steps downhill were more stable. I was less likely to miss my landing, jar a rock free, or slide on loose gravel. And, as with going uphill, many small steps are cumulatively less tiring than fewer big ones ...* ~ (Khadka, RS, *Travelers' Tales Nepal: True Stories of Life on the Road,* Travelers' Tales, 2000.)

There were days when we would walk for seven hours and only cover two kilometres as the crow flew. Walking over long distances became an enchantment, stitching environment and people together as we moved down, down, down into the valley below. Then straight up to a point higher than where we'd made camp the night before.

Don't Pat the Yaks—Nepal ~ 2009 ~

All to be seen were a little row of orange tents like pin pricks in the distance below.

The porters moved like magnificent, well-oiled machines. They carried incredible weights of up to and sometimes more than fifty kilograms, at altitude, risking their lives along narrow ridges with deadly drops below. Their sinewy bodies moved rhythmically at an unvarying pace in plastic thongs, scuffs or crumbling sand shoes. They rejected sturdy walking boots offered many times by travellers or expedition groups, preferring instead to be exposed to air and earth.

Our legendary porters

Trekking Nepal is a euphoric experience, when organised properly. Although we appeared to be cutting swathes through rarely tracked territory, we were in the expert care of World Expeditions who did

The World is Your Pearl

their research well for adventure travel, and were renowned for navigating small groups through the earth's most remote wilderness areas in ethical ways.

They had many commendable humanitarian and environmental policies. Although their porters were immensely strong, their loads were kept to a maximum of 30 to 40 kilograms, where some companies allowed varying loads of 50 to 80 kilograms per man.

Supplied were our kit bags, down jackets, sleeping bags and a crew of thirty men, including guides, Sherpas, cooks and porters who carried tents, stoves, chairs, tables, food and fuel. They easily arrived before us, up and down the mountains under all that weight, singing with smiles on their faces, while many Westerners would sometimes grimace under the hardship. Not only did they pride themselves on beating us to the campsite, but had tents pitched,

Don't Pat the Yaks—Nepal ~ 2009 ~

the mess tent erected, tables and chairs set out, and a hot drink ready for our arrival, with them nowhere to be seen, hidden away in another tent, cooking our evening meal.

Every night our aluminium drink bottles were filled with boiling water for us to insert into a sock to warm our sleeping bags. The next day we drank it on the trek. Around sunrise we received a tin mug of hot sweet tea through the flap of each tent, followed by a bowl of hot water, to the shout of, "Washy washy!"

From breakfast and beyond, all our food was hearty, and heaps of it.

We started out early the next morning to trek from Australia Camp to Landrung, which took us to altitude 5379 feet. The rain from the day before had cleared and the morning was clear and bright. The snow-capped Machhapuchhre (Fishtail) Mountains before us were dazzling, breathtaking glaciers, which glistened against the sky. We walked overland and up through almost vertical terraced peaks and down into valleys through farms where people worked with ancient implements.

It was like the Disney scene of Happy Valley. Many of the goats, donkeys and cows had bells around their necks. And placid water buffalo worked in the rice terraces. All were content and well fed. Hens with clutches of chicks pecked the ground. It was an idyllic scene where animals were well cared for in shelters with fresh straw.

The houses and paths were built over many centuries, from millions of stones shaped into blocks, and set into place over the high mountain passes. The signature colour of woodwork and windows everywhere was freshly painted blue and turquoise. Natural springs were tapped, and water ran continuously from pipes on the hillsides onto neatly concreted communal areas.

The World is Your Pearl

The Nepalese people appeared to have nothing, yet seemed to be some of the happiest on earth.

With seemingly little or no creature comforts they appeared to live happily in good health at altitude, often in temperatures many degrees below zero. They were warmly clothed, well fed, respectful, calm, kind, strong and operated in comfortable community with each other. There was almost no internet access in the remote parts of Nepal at the time of our trek in 2009, and it seemed that not many young people owned cellphones.

They regarded the pursuit of happiness as serious business. For the people on the land, working was their happiness. They went to their fields every day to grow everything they ate: garlic, rice, vegetables, corn and grains.

I once read about a lady named **Woeser Choeden**. She was 90 years old and had no formal education. In 1960 she fled Tibet to go to Nepal on foot with her four daughters. Two yaks carried the family food, as well as her two youngest daughters. She had 20 grandchildren and 10 great-grandchildren.

In her words:

> ~ *"Happiness is relative. There are always worries and failures, but I gather internal strength from the blessings of His Holiness the Dalai Lama. My life has been long. I find great happiness in having raised four independent and capable daughters. I am lucky. Happiness for me is about contentment, not about extremes of happiness or sadness. I tell my children to embrace the suffering and hardship that comes through hard work. Only then can one truly understand happiness"* ~ (https://www.wnpr.org/post/happiness-day-6-nepalis-tell-how-not-worry-and-be-happy, accessed August 1, 2020.)

Don't Pat the Yaks—Nepal ~ 2009 ~

Arriving at Landrung, our tents were already pitched, as was the mess tent where hot tea and coffee were ready. A few of us assembled to do some yoga stretches while looking out over terraces cascading for miles below. Dennis hurt his ankle as he played ball with some children. It was sudden: *now you see him, now you don't!* Running backwards to catch the ball, he disappeared over the edge, falling 10 feet into a vegetable patch in the terrace below. Luckily the injury wasn't severe, though for the next couple of days he walked in some pain.

There were various tea houses and vendors here and there, selling beer. A few of us bought beers and sat on wooden benches, seemingly on top of the world, in the fading light. We chatted and laughed while enjoying the view of endless terraces across the valley. Back in the mess tent we ate dinner and played a few card games before heading off to get an early night. The long days of walking in the fresh mountain air sent me into a deep and satisfying sleep each night.

The walk the next day towards Ghandrung took us five hours, but would only have been a distance of a kilometre as the crow flew. As we left our tent camp, we followed a steep trail downwards through rice terraces for over an hour to the base of the valley. We crossed a steel bridge over the glacial Modi Khola River, then ascended the many stone staircases, straight up, for a further four hours.

Our reward when we arrived was the luxury of solar-heated showers and accommodations in the cute little Ghandrung Lodge at an altitude of 6726 feet, which overlooked vast expanses of mountain ranges. A few of us did some yoga stretches on a small walled terrace. Looking down, we could see a little row of orange dots far beneath us in the distance. These were the permanent tents we had camped in the night before.

One of our friends was Gael, a yoga instructor. It became a ritual for her to lead some of us each morning and evening to perform yoga. It was a glorious morning, and after salutes to the sun and a gorgeous breakfast of porridge, eggs and tomatoes, we left the main trail and walked in bright sunshine towards Tadapani.

We trekked higher and higher for eight hours through glorious jungle vegetation dripping with orchids and moss, and on through ancient forests of magnolias and rhododendrons. When we came to creeks and gorges, the mosses were exquisite in their intricacies. At one point I stopped to photograph the shiny shells of a loveliness of sixty to a hundred ladybirds. There were thousands of them everywhere on the mossy rocks.

We walked on quietly, in anticipation of spotting some monkeys.

Along the way, we chatted to some Germans who were passing through. They told us they had flown direct into Tenzing Hillary Airport in Lukla. This was the gateway to Mount Everest at an elevation of 9383 feet. They had intended to start their trek from there. But instead of trekking, they'd spent 24 hours flat on their backs with severe headaches.

> ~ Note: ~
> *This trek can't realistically be done in reverse as the sudden effect of altitude has such a debilitating effect. The easier option is to acclimatise gradually by climbing in increments upwards to where the air is thinner.*

Our lunch was cooked and served by our own crew in a small tea house along the path. We rested on wooden benches in the sun, and enjoyed the view, before continuing for a further two hours. Passing little waterfalls which cascaded down the narrow gullies, we arrived in Tadapani, where we camped in a clearing in the forest, at an altitude of 8694 feet.

Don't Pat the Yaks—Nepal ~ 2009 ~

In the town, there were locals selling various knitted yak wool socks, hats, blankets and scarves from small stalls along the street. After dinner in the mess tent, we had an early night.

Our group was fabulous. We laughed and joked and chatted constantly. The thread of my drink bottle lid died. Paul was able to fix it with a piece of string and a bandage.

Ascending higher and higher the next morning, we journeyed for four hours to Dobato at an altitude 11,300 feet. Along the way, the clouds darkened the sky and it began to snow as our crew fixed a hot lunch served on a big ground sheet. We drank hot cordial, and ate chicken and vegetable soup, a hot vegetable dish of carrots, cabbage, onions and garlic, and toasted tomato and yak cheese sandwiches. As we chatted about yak cheese, our guide told us to be sure to stay away from the yaks.

On a previous trek one woman saw a wild yak and, unbelievably, wandered over to pat it. These beasts could weigh as much as 800 to 1000 kilograms. Their horns were very large. The yak became spooked by the woman, and swung his huge head down and twisted with a wild swing, bringing its substantial horn up to gore her straight through the fleshy part of her inner thigh. She was lifted into the air, screaming, as he took off with her, flipping and flailing around before she was dropped, with blood everywhere. She was in a very bad way. They had to strap the wound very tightly and the Sherpas carried her down the mountain in this gory state for two days before they could connect with any form of help. It must have been terrifying for everyone to see and monstrously painful for her.

Altitude gave us all headaches. They came and went as we acclimatised.

We traversed a landslide which went down around 1000 feet, caused, we were told, by soil erosion due to deforestation.

The World is Your Pearl

Towards Dobato, Annapurna Region – Nepal
Photos from Dennis Dawson and Mike Litchfield

Don't Pat the Yaks—Nepal ~ 2009 ~

The skies darkened further and eventually we were walking through thick snow. Higher and higher the paths became narrower and more treacherous. A spectacular thunder and lightning storm set in. The ground shuddered beneath us as ear-splitting thunder clapped around us, and lightning lit up the snowy scene in a dazzling display.

The trail began to peter out as we followed our guides. From the kits they were carrying, they produced little digging devices which they used to chop out a makeshift ledge. Using their feet at the same time, they stamped out a foot-wide trail along the steep slope of snow which dropped away to 2000 feet below.

This precarious section lasted an hour and a half. With nothing to hold on to, it played havoc with my vertigo. The way was relentless and seemed never-ending. Around every bend there was another expanse of icy ledges, which became more treacherous by the minute. With thunder cracking and lightning flashing, we commenced our descent into the campsite.

Fifteen minutes before we arrived, our friend Paul was struck down by a charge from the corona of lightning. He felt the crack to his head and the electricity go through him. I must have been ahead or behind, as I didn't see it happen. However, the timing was both good and bad. Bad that it had happened at all, but good because one more step by Paul into the direct path of the lightning strike, could have been disastrous. He could easily have been killed. By the time we arrived at our camp in Dobato, he was pretty sick and woozy.

Our tents had been set up in a clearing in front of a mountain lodge. They were standing in a row, steadily being covered in snow. They went unused except for those used by Birbal, Sirdar, and Sherpas Maila and Thering. We had been fortunate, and very grateful to be offered beds and the use of an indoor toilet inside the mountain lodge.

The World is Your Pearl

Snow camp – Dobato

This had been our hardest day. The weather was unseasonable for this time of year. The snow was completely unexpected as there wasn't usually any snowfall here in March. Each day, there seemed to be a pattern of sun in the morning, gradually closing in, to rain and cold in the latter part of the afternoons. Today's trek was ranked in the travel notes at a level of difficulty of two. However, because of the extreme change in weather conditions, we were told ours turned out to be ranked at level four.

A black Labrador had followed us all the way from Tadapani. We named him 'Warby'. He slept in the snow and followed us every day, enjoying scraps from our camp cooks. The late Sherpa mountaineer Tenzing Norgay said that having a black dog accompanying you is especially good luck. I guess we were lucky that Paul hadn't been killed by the lightning.

Don't Pat the Yaks—Nepal ~ 2009 ~

The kitchen dining area inside the lodge had been warmed from a fire lit in a potbellied stove, improvised from a 40 gallon drum. We placed our boots around it to dry, and hung wet gear wherever we could, then played Yahtzee by the light of a kerosene lamp until dinner time. Dinner was a magnificent meal of a large assortment of flavoursome and hearty vegetarian dishes, pasta with mushrooms, garlic and herbs, and flatbreads.

It had been a long day. Gael shared a room with me. We were so tired, we crawled into our sleeping bags in our clothes. Everyone was exhausted and we all slept for eleven hours.

We woke the next morning as though emerging from a hibernation into bright sunshine. Icicles dripped from the roof of the lodge which regularly dropped sheets of snow outside our window. Shuffling down the hallway, I saw Birbal outside, digging the snow off their tents with a tray. The boys had taken down our tents last night to save time in the morning due to the weather.

We packed easily and ate another sumptuous breakfast before setting out in the pristine snow, followed by our dog Warby. The sun was glorious, and we soon peeled off the layers as we moved steadily down the mountainside. After a couple of hours, the trail turned upwards for a further 2623 feet to our next camp at Christibung at 10,335 feet.

Our Sherpas must have been carrying incredible weight, made heavy by the wet tents from the night before. Although they were slight of build, they were sinewy, powerfully strong, ever smiling, and often singing in their work.

We had walked for six hours with a break for a hot picnic lunch on the side of the mountain. Everything was carried, and pots and pans came out often to provide warming meals. Once again, by the time we arrived, our tents were in place. The camp had

The World is Your Pearl

been set up on a flat ridge with a spectacular view of 2000 feet below.

It turned freezing cold in the afternoon as the snow began to fall again.

We sat together in the mess tent, reading, writing, playing cards and chatting before dinner at 6:30, and were early to bed.

Throughout the night, our tents were beaten several times with sticks by the crew, both before and after we went to bed as the snow continued to fall. This would have ensured we weren't buried in it. Then all was silent.

Many hours later the call of nature required me to leave the warmth of my cosy tent, and crawl out into the night, to icy temperatures of five degrees below zero. I was struck with awe by the stunning fairyland lacework of trees, completely covered in snow. These were made all the more spectacular by the contrast of a vast, velvety black night sky, suspended with billions of twinkling stars, many of them large, the likes of which I'd never seen anywhere before.

Our table groaned under the weight of our breakfast once again in the morning. Every meal throughout the trek was three courses, full of variety, hearty, hot and heaps of it. We sat down to a choice of porridge, muesli, granola, pancakes with maple syrup, sugar and lemon. Flatbreads with a choice of marmalade, jam, peanut butter, Nutella or vegemite, and hot chocolate, tea or coffee were served.

This was to be fuel for a climb of 2625 feet to our camp at Kopre Ridge.

Although it was snowing, freezing and wet, we were buoyed up with adrenaline as we navigated our way through this land of remote

Don't Pat the Yaks—Nepal ~ 2009 ~

beauty. The laughter which resounded constantly throughout the group, day and night, on this trip was a load of fun.

At one point, around a particularly heart-stopping precipice, Birbal, a highly accomplished Sherpa, held my hand because of my horrendous issues with vertigo, and fed me along many of the ledges, saying, "Don't be frightened." The snow was soft powder, which packed as we trod. The Sherpas made snowballs and rolled them down the mountainside.

They got bigger and bigger. Then petered out. I asked, "If one of us went over, would we slow, like the snowball?" He said, "No, we are heavier ... just keep going." I then asked him if we could be easily rescued. His answer ... "Maybe not." These were questions I shouldn't have asked while freaking out on the edge of a precipice.

Once, when we stopped in a safe place to wait for the others (still holding hands), Paul yelled out, "Are you two getting married?" I said, "After this ... he's all mine."

This must have pleased Birbal, as, on another ledge after a tea break, I said, "Where's my man?" He said, "Your man is here!"

Birbal came from the Everest region and also worked as a Sherpa for trekkers on Mount Everest. With a wife and a little six-year-old boy, his life was hard, but he was grateful for the work, and appeared to enjoy it immensely. He took pride in knowing everyone was happy. All Sherpas spent many months at a time away from their families. It was an incredibly tough life.

Our leader, Subal, had been very concerned by the sudden change of weather conditions. It had turned into a full-blown blizzard, and we were too high up to turn back.

The World is Your Pearl

We eventually reached Kopre summit. Eight degrees below zero, with no power and no fire except in the stone hut where the cooks made our food. We couldn't really go in there. The man who ran the lodge must have trekked up just to open it for us because of the blizzard. Although our tents had been pitched in the snow, we were lucky, once again, to be able to sleep inside the lodge for the night. I didn't fancy sleeping in the deep snow and howling winds up here.

I asked for a dish of water, had a hot wash and got into some dry clothes, but didn't feel much warmer. We huddled together inside a round stone hut with wooden floors and a wood shingled roof and were all ready for bed by 2:00 p.m. Many had an afternoon nap before tea and biscuits at 4:00 p.m.

The food was truly amazing. That night we ate soup, veggies, rice, fried egg, and tomato stew. The head cook came out personally with a huge 'celebration cake'. It was a dense, freshly made lemon cake, with a creamy white icing, "for reaching the summit".

The Sherpas carry everything to the top. Dozens of eggs, kero for cooking, fresh vegetables, flour, rice, canned fruit, stove, dining tables and chairs, our tents, the mess tent, the toilet tent and seat, wash stand with Dettol soap on a string. Pots and pans, dishes and cutlery all scrubbed and shiny.

After dinner, cocooned in everything I could wear, I struggled into my bed in one of the tiny rooms of the cabin. This was much easier than the struggle would have been into a tent. Here I slept on a foam mattress in the sleeping bag in all my clothes, including thermals, polar fleece, socks, plastic jacket and pants, with the down jacket on top around my shoulders, and with the addition of a ski neck scarf and holding on tightly to my hot water bottle in a sock.

Don't Pat the Yaks—Nepal ~ 2009 ~

The walls of the hut were made of tin and covered with woven bamboo. It was so utterly freezing we could see the breath coming out of our mouths.

It was still dark when I woke at 5:30 a.m. I sat up in bed wrapped in the down jacket and wrote in my journal by the light of my head torch until a hot cup of tea arrived, brought in by one of the porters. I was not looking forward to returning around the snow and ice ledges.

Our leaders had been even more concerned at the extreme weather conditions. With no idea of how bad it was going to get, and fearing that we could all become trapped and snowed in for weeks, they made the decision to abandon the further climbs and return with haste as far down the mountain as we could go in one day.

That day was to be an extremely long trek. After breakfast we left Kopre Ridge at 8:00 a.m. Subal and Birbal flanked me front and back. However, it turned out not to be as harrowing as I'd anticipated. With only a few extreme panic moments, we eventually got to more open snow where Birbal could let go of my hand.

Stopping for lunch at Christibung, our previous 'fairyland' camp had now thawed to a square patch of snow. We sat in the sun on a plastic tarp. This was an ecstatic moment. With the sun warming my back and the most dangerous leg of the journey clearly behind me, I was feeling elated.

Throughout all its varying degrees of difficulty, every part of this trek was breathtakingly beautiful in the crisp mountain air. I felt very much at one with nature. It was a great privilege to be here amongst forests of rhododendrons where two species of monkeys lived. In this area, there were red pandas and beautiful snow leopards, but so rare as to be almost non-existent. Sadly, we saw neither.

The World is Your Pearl

We traversed steadily downwards all day. At one point we could see a group of people far below us in the distance. We cooeed out to them, but got no answer. Always the jokester, Dennis yelled down, "Don't come up here, there's only three of us left, we've got no toes!"

We travelled through jungles down a steep descent where I needed help on a long rocky ledge which fell away to the valley below. Warby the dog barked at three monkeys as they swung away through the trees.

Over eight hours we'd descended 4593 feet, and arrived at the small village of Swanta at 4:00 p.m.

We ate dinner by candlelight in a little tea house which had no power due to the storm. The laughter emitting from our group was always enough to light up the mountainside. It went on for a bit longer after I'd crawled into the tent that night and slept.

A few hours later I woke in the night to a tiny mouse which ran around my head and neck. I sat up with my head torch to look for it. In the morning when I dragged out my sleeping bag, I must have rolled on him in the night because there he was, as dead as a doornail, as flat as a tack. It appeared to be a weeny antechinus, or some equivalent marsupial. Subal said these usually grow over a foot long, and to wash my hands. So I guessed it must have been a rat. Even so, I was saddened by its unfortunate demise. Kev told everyone over breakfast, "It was flatter than a shit carter's hat."

I felt great this morning as I'd woken at 5:30 a.m. without a headache for the first time in several days. Because of our drop in altitude, everyone was feeling much better, and my writing flowed more easily when the fingers weren't frozen.

We left at 8:30 a.m. and walked for four and a half hours, accompanied by Warby the dog. He had followed us for five days.

Don't Pat the Yaks—Nepal ~ 2009 ~

Then, as suddenly as he'd joined us, he abandoned us to join up with another group.

We walked back into civilisation along a very pretty uphill track, through farm villages. Passing a house being built by four men. A little girl stood in tattered rags with her grandfather, her hair in pigtails. Another man held a tiny naked baby in the sunshine as he walked around helping the others. The people lived in a rock bottom economy. The young boys worked as Sherpas while trying to study in between at college. Many were clever enough for university, but unable to afford it, they had no way to get ahead.

Our lodge at Goropani was comfortable but spartan, like everywhere in Nepal. It was built of thin plywood packing cases. A little bit of carpet in the rooms was a surprise and quite a luxury. I snagged a 'hot' shower for 100 rupees (AU$2) downstairs in the dungeon which was pitch dark but for a tiny window. On this occasion, their water had to be heated by a wood-fired furnace as there was no electricity. Lightning had blown up the transformer when we were on the ridge to Dobato days before and the entire region had been without power ever since. They had no infrastructure as back-up.

The sound ecological policies of World Expeditions meant that they didn't patronise tea house accommodations who used wood fires to heat their water. These methods caused deforestation, including the felling of massive hundred-year-old rhododendrons and varieties of ancient trees at an alarming rate.

On our second day at Goropani, we were woken with a cup of tea at 4:30 a.m. I hadn't slept for the constant barking of many big dogs all night.

We left the lodge to walk in the freezing cold temperature of around three degrees, wearing four layers of clothes, hats and gloves. We were soon stinking hot, but would be frozen without them. In the pitch dark I looked back at the long line of head torches like a procession of fireflies or miners coming up out of the earth.

We were setting out for one of the memorable highlights of the trip on a 45-minute walk up Poon Hill to climb a tower and watch the sunrise over the glaciers of the Annapurna Himalayan Range before breakfast. We arrived at the summit of 10,450 feet just as daylight was breaking to a piercing purple sky. As the sun peeked from behind us, it lit up the glaciers in colours of pinks and apricots, foiled with icy blues, aquas and mauves. Its beauty made me want to cry.

We stood there, enraptured as the sun worked its magic before our eyes. It was like looking through a sparkling kaleidoscope, and utterly breathtaking. By the time the sun rose, many dozens of people had arrived, and surprise, surprise, curled up in a ball at the base of the tower was Warby dog. Our professional beggar had found his way and must have been one of last night's 'barkers'.

Mules filed through the town, loaded up with stones and wood. They were unloaded outside our tea house and issued with numbered nosebags. They tossed their heads back to get the last bits. The mules are a crossbreed between a donkey and a horse. I learned that they are sterile and can never breed. A female horse and a male donkey have a mule. But hinnies and mules can't have babies of their own. They have trouble making sperm or eggs because their chromosomes don't match up well.

A donkey can carry four times its own weight. A mule can carry even more. Later we saw unsaddled mules with the fur rubbed off their backs and open sores, the poor things.

The following morning we set out in high spirits to walk for six hours towards Hille on a steep descent down, down, down. Although very hard on the knees, we were jollied along with conversations and a bit of song singing. We passed processions of up to a hundred mules with bells on their necks to the sounds of 'ding da ding da ding-a-ling'. They wore lovely woven saddle rugs and ornate triangular brow pieces with tassels.

Suddenly we were on a trail teeming with tourists from all over the world. We ate lunch in the sun at a table in a cafe on the side of a mountain. Fourteen of us at one table and around thirty French people on two other tables. They were singing French songs. We started to sing 'Waltzing Matilda'. This caused a 'sing off'. They loved it and joined in as we struck up with rounds of 'Frère Jacques', then they sang 'Clementine'. The whole mountain resounded with our voices as everyone sang together drinking Everest Beer.

After lunch at the cafe, we continued on a tough trail downward, thankful for the aid of the walking poles as we passed a universal mecca of Japanese, Dutch, Korean, German, English, Thai, French and American tourists on their way up on a day hike.

We arrived in Hille around 3:00 p.m. Our tents were at the ready for our last night of camping. Just as I blew up the mattress, laid out the sleeping bag and its liner, washed my feet and treated a blister, did a few stretches then walked up to the tea house dining room for afternoon tea, *down came the rain!*

We sat reading, writing, playing cards, drinking beer and planning a party for the departure from our crew. We took up a collection of tips which we handed out that night to the Sherpas, porters, guides and cooks, along with speeches. Then we sang and danced to some recorded Nepalese music. They had seen us through this remarkable trek in safety and comfort.

None of us wanted this trip to end. We walked out for the last time, along a magnificent river's edge where the water was crystal clear, and rushing over smooth rocks. There were people fishing with sledgehammers. They whacked and whacked the big rocks to stun the fish as they swam past, then placed them in a net. The tiny fish were only two to three inches long but we were told they were very sweet to eat.

Before reaching Kande we went through a town where the cable bridge had been taken out at one end by a landslide. We had to crawl under the shops and climb down the cliff side to traverse the river below where a board crossing had been erected. Luckily it wasn't monsoon season.

The bus to Kande nearly shook to bits over the huge potholes. It was called a *Disco Video Bus* and was *very* ornate with frilly curtains, disco lights in its panelled ceiling of pressed metal, and fancy floral insets of plastic flowers which shivered and shook as we hurtled down the mountainside with brakes screeching metal on metal, as we headed back to Pokarah.

The roads were really bad. Unsealed, deeply potholed and rough with rubble. We crossed muddy landslides with great gaping holes where much of the road had been eroded or washed away, often allowing no passing space. The soil was barren and stony.

The architecture here was diverse in its structure. The people built from whatever they could find and everything was put to use. Steel mesh stuck out of concrete blocks and house bricks, while bamboo, plywood and packing cases made up the rest. Each roof was made of tin, and held on with many large rocks. Any building or construction was made using ancient implements. Planks were made by hand with axes, adzes and planes. Cuts were made by two men on either side of a saw. Drains were made by groups of men, slicing out sections of long lengths of bamboo. Everything was labour-intensive and seemingly uneconomical.

Don't Pat the Yaks—Nepal ~ 2009 ~

Arriving in Pokarah, our bus skirted around cows walking up and down the streets, scavenging in rubbish bins as the traffic of cars, trucks and bikes moved around them.

Once settled into our hotel we had free time. Half our group went off to hire bikes to go off on an 80-kilometre ride. It was a local bike hire business and the bikes turned out to be cheap and extremely inferior. Our friends experienced nothing but trouble with bike gears that didn't work, ratchets which just gave up and spun on the spot offering no forward motion, and multiple punctures. Others of the group took rowboats to cross the lake to an island where they climbed for an hour to visit a white stupa at the top.

It was extremely hot and steamy and I decided to veg out for the day to catch up on washing and just mosey around the town where there were shops full of cottage industries. Strolling around, it was interesting to look at stalls selling embroidered cushions, mats, clothes and bags. Others sold elaborate earrings and jewellery of coral, turquoise, lapis lazuli, agate and gemstones. There was also an array of cashmere pashminas and yak wool jumpers, socks and hats, leather belts and purses.

I sat in a cafe and ate bruschetta with a cup of ginger tea, while reading my book to the sounds of Led Zeppelin.

The following morning we commenced our return to Kathmandu. After breakfast on the rooftop of the hotel, our red World Expeditions bags were loaded on top of the Video Bus which was parked on the grass next to two families picnicking next to their Winnebagos. I was inspired to learn that they had been travelling from their homes in Germany for six months with their little kids and their bicycles, pushers and play pens.

We flew to Kathmandu on Yeti Airlines where we were issued with cotton wool for our ears, lollies and a paper cup with a half measure of black coffee. Security at Pokhara and Kathmandu airports was hilarious. Every bag was checked by unzipping, then guards' hands plopped around on top. Nothing was removed. Ladies were sent to the left, men to the right to be frisked behind a curtain. No doubt things will have changed dramatically since this time in 2009.

The air pollution wasn't so bad in Kathmandu on our return seventeen days after our first arrival. Major petrol shortages had resulted in violent street demonstrations, including the use of explosives, and necessitating the posting of travel warnings to Kathmandu. This meant that less cars, trucks and bikes had been on the roads, resulting in less smog. Now, as we inched along, there must have been 500 motorbikes, taxis and cars, lined up for hours as far as the eye could see. I couldn't imagine waiting all day in the hot sun, then getting there just as the fuel ran out.

There was not much infrastructure in Kathmandu. Their electrical power was limited to just four hours a day. A machinist worked at a sewing machine, embroidering t-shirts in the hours of power, then attempted to sell them in the afternoon by candlelight in his blacked-out shop.

Our last meal in Kathmandu was in the famous Rum Doodle restaurant, a mecca where all the mountaineers went. Anyone who summited Mount Everest received their meal for free. The atmosphere was great, with thousands of Yeti footprints covering the walls and ceilings throughout with details of expeditions. I prepared a footprint for the Warby Ghostriders (including Warby dog). Everyone signed it; Paul added himself as 'Lightning Jack' and it was nailed up in a prominent place. We ate, drank, danced and partied on into the night.

We returned by rickshaw in the rain. One of our friends, whose name was also Rick, pushed from the back as the boy pedalled, everyone laughing on adrenaline. My white dress was covered in mud, road grime, red wine, bat shit from the trees above. We'd had a ball. I was sad to learn in 2020 that the Rum Doodle no longer exists.

This trip showed me how easy it was to go somewhere off the beaten track to see the world in safety with all the hard work taken out of it. Our organisers had previously sussed out the route, provided crews, provisions, transport, guides, excellent equipment and ensured an incredible experience. This had been the only way to go.

Kathmandu was crazy, hot and dry but life hummed along with a rhythm like no other. The ancient wood and red earth buildings contrasted with the dazzlingly vivid colour combinations of women in their beautiful pristine saris.

A holy man was painted with ash all over his body with symbolic colours displayed on his forehead. His hair was in dreadlocks as long as himself. He sat poised, with one leg behind his head, wearing just a loin cloth, in a temple doorway.

Having come from such a sheltered existence, it was a shock for me to see so many beggars everywhere. Little children asked for money for food, or sat in the street with their baby brother or sister, in rags, asleep in the hot sun, next to begging bowls. Lots of skeletal men with matted hair slept on the roadside in rags, their dark skin blackened further by road grime.

Women holding babies asked passersby for milk to feed them. Holding up an empty baby's bottle, saying, "No money, just milk, madam, to feed the baby." They were everywhere. It was heartbreaking. I felt overwhelmed that I couldn't help them.

A friend later told me that she'd had this experience in India. It was explained to her, after she'd bought some milk for an Indian

The World is Your Pearl

lady, that an agreement was arranged between the beggar and the shop owner. You buy the milk for the beggar. The beggar takes it back to the shop after you leave, and the shop owner gives her half the price of the milk.

That made more sense, and seemed a perfect arrangement where everyone would win. Whatever the circumstances, they went about their daily lives with quiet dignity.

The dominant feature of society in Nepal was their sense of unity as they lived among the diverse customs, practices and beliefs of major religions between Hinduism, Buddhism, Islam and Christianity.

They held on to their faith through festivals and sacrifice. We walked past the carcasses of two young water buffalo, freshly slaughtered as a sacrifice outside an altar. Blood poured out everywhere all over the pavement and onto the road as women passed gracefully by in their beautiful saris. Incense burned along the streets, as dirt, rubbish, melted wax and the black ash from burned offerings contrasted with a vibrant sea of marigolds and mixed flowers.

CHAPTER 7

The Ringleader of My Adventures

(A bad cycling day)

~ Difficult roads can often lead to beautiful destinations ~

My brother Steve was my only sibling. He was the eagle who soared above me, and the biggest influence on me as I grew up. He was a hugely popular man with his own sense of self who never cared what anyone thought of him. He was three years younger than me but we were close, and I loved him. Everyone loved him. He was gorgeous-looking, tall, dark and handsome. A real head-turner, completely unconscious of his good looks and personality. Our mother loved noting the stares he received as she walked down the street with him. He was a cross in features between Rock Hudson, George Clooney and Eric Bana.

The World is Your Pearl

Steve and Glenda in the 1980s

He was adventurous, capable and such fun to be with. I loved being around him. As children, playing with other kids, he was the King of the Castle and we were all the dirty rascals. He swept everyone along with his enthusiasm and daredevil approach to life, and was my springboard to trying new experiences. As we grew up, I always felt safe with him doing things I wouldn't normally dream of doing. Picking our way around dangerous cliffs and crevices, co-piloting the planes he jumped out of as a skydiver, water skiing, snow skiing, flying with him in his plane, and standing up behind him on the back of his powerful jet ski, taking my breath away as it went from 0 to 100 kph in 5 seconds.

He was a natural leader of men. At the age of 21 he joined the Australian Army Reserves artillery corps, and became a bombardier.

Moving to Papua New Guinea, he worked for the mining company Bougainville Copper Limited for seven years. While there he studied and obtained his pilot's licence, and whenever he came home on leave he'd hire a sea plane and take me to Tipplers Tavern on South Stradbroke Island, where we'd land on the water and taxi in amongst the beautiful yachts and cruisers. On returning

The Ringleader of My Adventures

permanently to Australia, he purchased his own Cessna aeroplane, naming it 'Teeny Weeny Airlines'.

I flew with him up and down the coast of Queensland. On one occasion we flew to Great Keppel Island. We always felt at ease in each other's company and talked and laughed constantly. We did some exploring around the island, had a few drinks at the resort, then slept under the wing of the plane before returning to the Gold Coast the next day.

Steve on Great Keppel Island

The World is Your Pearl

By now he could probably have retired, but he was only in his late 20s, and always needed a reason to get up in the morning. Highly qualified with twelve different licences to operate any super machinery from cranes to excavators, he became a master of anything he was asked to do in heavy operations, and went to work on high-rise buildings all over Queensland's Gold Coast. Loving life, he took pride in everything he did, and over the next 20 years, amassed a considerable amount of money by his sheer hard work and astuteness with life choices.

He was an utterly spontaneous being, a regular skydiver and scuba diver. Weekends were often spent in his tinny, fishing and camping on the islands with his army mate Wally; he had a lovely girlfriend called Kate, and life was good.

It happened on the day of the Winter Solstice, June 21, 2008. I lived in Melbourne, and was leaving for a bike ride with the Warby Ghostriders. I had a huge day planned where, following the morning ride, I would head home to get ready to go to an afternoon movie with friends so I'd be parked in Belgrave for the first Winter Solstice Lantern Parade through the main street (where the whole town of Belgrave would be blocked off that night). I had a table booked downstairs at La Collina, our favourite Italian restaurant, for 17 friends to have an early dinner and by 7:00 p.m. it would be time to join the parade.

That morning, our cycling group were to ride from Pakenham to Drouin and back. A round trip of 75 kilometres. My friend Gael, a fellow rider, picked me up from home, and with our bikes on the back of her car, we headed to Pakenham.

I phoned Lisa, another rider who lives in Pakenham, to see if she was joining us. She said, "Are you kidding? It's pouring here." She was still in bed. As we neared Pakenham, on either side of us the sky was a murky grey green, which could be classified as

The Ringleader of My Adventures

an end-of-the-earth, doomsday colour. But the highway we drove along was blasting with bright sunlight. I phoned Lisa back and said she should come because it was clear and sunny. But it was still pouring with rain at her house. She was curling up with a book. When we got to the start point, we were the only ones there, so we set out alone in the sun and had a fabulous ride.

The ritual for all riders was to head to a coffee shop or bakery where everyone propped their bikes outside and, in their yellow Ghostrider jerseys and lycra nicks, *'take over the joint'*. Many times there could be more than 20 of us. As we sat there alone, who should come walking across the road in their yellow jerseys but our 'head honcho' Dennis Dawson, and another rider, Pete. As they walked in, I said, "You dirty dogs—CHEATING!" Ha ha ha.

The weather was so bad where they lived that they decided to drive out and do the reverse ride. We had coffees and the boys had vanilla slices and buns because *'they only ride to eat'*! Then the four of us headed back, laughing and chatting, as I received two consecutive phone calls. As my phone rang in my pocket the first time, I stopped to take the call. Gael waited for me and the others kept going. After dealing with the first call, Gael and I set out to catch up with the others when the phone rang again. As I slowed to take the second call, I told Gael to keep going and I would catch up. When I answered it was my mum in Queensland. I knew something was wrong as she never called me, it was always me who phoned her (due to my busy life).

As I stood on the side of the road in the middle of nowhere, Mum said, "Steven's been killed." Police officers had just knocked on her door to tell her the news. My legs buckled from under me and I dropped to the ground as she described that the scaffold he'd been working on had given way and he had fallen 27 storeys to his death. He'd been killed doing the thing he loved best. A good day's work.

The World is Your Pearl

I couldn't talk. I hung up in shock and was on the ground, crying alone, when a young driver stopped to see if I was all right. He had his little two-year-old son in the back and they were heading to a BBQ in the opposite direction. However, he helped me into the front seat of his Ute, put my bike on the back, did a U-turn, collected Gael and her bike along the way, and, passing to explain to Dennis and Pete, took us both to Gael's car in Pakenham.

His name was Daniel Argoon, and he'd driven miles out of his way in this generous act of kindness. The same could be said for Gael and her husband Gerry, who skipped the rest of the day's planned activities, drove me home to pack, collected Emma from her apartment in East Melbourne, and drove us all the way to the airport for our flight to Queensland.

Mum was in a mess when I phoned her back. She told me it had happened that morning. Steve had arrived at her place at 5:30 a.m. It was his ritual to go in and make her a cuppa in bed and have his breakfast, two coffees and a long chat every morning before heading off to start work by 7:00 a.m. He cared for her well and would never leave her as she aged, not even to come down to visit me in Melbourne. Down the track his plan was always for us to travel on adventures around the world together once Mum's time here was done.

This day Steve was working on a building in Broadbeach. The boss called him over and asked him to finish rendering the outside of the 27th floor, as the person who was supposed to be working on it was being inducted onto the site of the new building next door. The workmate he was sent up to assist was Chris, a young man with a wife and two small children.

Steve and Chris had been working downwards from the top floor for two hours as the scaffold was lowered by cables attached to the counterweights above. Suddenly, one counterweight

The Ringleader of My Adventures

gave way and came off the top of the building and the platform dropped, suspended from one side with the two men hanging from harnesses. They screamed out, but because the building was almost completed, the cranes had already been removed and taken to the next site. There was no time to reach them before the second counterweight gave way and they plummeted to their deaths at the same moment that I was cycling 2000 kilometres away through the blasting sunshine surrounded by the black-green skies on either side.

Reports said that the crashing sound reverberated all over the Gold Coast. It was a most traumatic way to lose him. One of the administrators explained to me that it was better this way than if they'd hung there for many minutes longer as they would have died excruciating deaths from the cut to circulation from the harnesses around their groins. There was only so long they could hold themselves up to take the pressure off.

The swinging scaffold was attached to the top of the high rise with counterweights. In every other state of Australia, the law stipulated that men must be harnessed to the building, but this didn't apply in Queensland. They were harnessed to the scaffold. Government legislation was changed as a result of this horrendous accident.

There were 800 people at his funeral. The military personnel and work bosses who spoke emphasised the high esteem in which he was held, calling him a diamond of a man and a true leader of men. I gave his eulogy.

It was a cathartic exercise to encapsulate his life in words, demanding the essence of his nature and life path to flood back, and be summarily described in a nutshell to be presented over a few minutes. Like the process of looking back through a photo album, it was a great privilege to conjure recollections of past experiences, how he evolved, who he influenced and the mark he left behind.

The World is Your Pearl

Bombardier Steve Sayer 1975

It became a cathartic process which required me to actually map the course of my own life at the same time. This thought process would be used in an absorbing way two years later to analyse the reasons why things went as they did.

Life switches and turns, like an ant walking the pattern of a Persian rug. It can follow the line of colour in one direction. It comes to an intersection. If it takes the path to the right its life will be directed one way. A decision to turn left could be a path leading under the shoe of a passerby.

The Ringleader of My Adventures

The course our lives take can be random or contrived. A 'yes' or a 'no' will determine the direction we will take. "Yes, I will marry you" or "No, I won't take that job". The path which others take can affect your own future too.

Steve's death caused me to do the 'Forrest Gump' and ride across the Nullarbor to Perth and back to Melbourne on a pushbike.

CHAPTER 8

Doing the Forrest Gump Across the Nullarbor
~ 2010 ~

Don't mess with the road trains—the legendary huge semi-trailers which can be over 53 metres long, 2.5 metres wide, weigh up to 125 tonnes and travel at 100 kph.

One day in 2010, I received a phone call from my dear friend Frank Hands; he was the manufacturing jeweller who made my engagement and wedding rings when Peter and I married 32 years before. After that, Frank and his wife Shirley became our lifetime family friends.

When Shirley died, Frank continued to visit, sometimes with his best mate, Bertie Lambshed. Bert was the renowned engraver asked by the Australian Federal Government to engrave a silver tray which formed part of the gifts from Australia to Prince Charles and Princess Diana when they married, and now resides in one of the royal houses.

The World is Your Pearl

Frank phoned: "I'm coming up to have lunch with you. I want to see you before I go." I asked him where he was off to. "Perth," he said. I asked him if he'd be flying or driving? He said, "Driving. And you'd be very welcome to come with me if you have a spare seven weeks!"

I thought, *Very funny, Frank. This to a person who never has two minutes to rub together.* He said, "Well, think about it; if you'd like to come you could bring your bike."

By the time Frank arrived I'd made up my mind to go. Why had I even hesitated? Steve had been killed suddenly at the age of 52, and none of us knew what was around the corner. Life was short. Frank danced around the kitchen like a school kid. He was ninety years old.

We discussed the prospect of making it a full cycling event as a fundraiser. He was thrilled with the idea. However, for me, there was one proviso regarding the ride. He had to be driving either 50 kilometres in front of me, or 50 kilometres behind, but not be sitting on my wheel all the way. It was agreed.

When Dennis, our fearless leader of the Warby Ghostriders, learned of my decision, he put me in touch with a couple of Ghostriders who had ridden around Australia the year before for charity. Karen and David Brown invited me to visit them in their home, where we pored over maps of where they'd ridden in aid of Australian Rotary Health in 2009. They were full of information, tips and tricks, dos and don'ts, describing hazards and road conditions in various places to watch out for, what to take, and ways of packing light.

My daughter Emma always made Mother's Day span a whole weekend in memorable ways. This year was to be spent together at the Satyananda Yoga retreat in the Rocklyn Ashram near

Doing the Forrest Gump Across the Nullarbor ~ 2010 ~

Daylesford. It was a quiet time of reflection, meditation, yoga and delicious vegetarian food. Afterwards, Em and I spent time together in Daylesford on Mother's Day, May 9, 2010.

After lunch, Frank met me in the main street driving his 1959, pillar-box-red Mercedes Benz, an ex-postal van which had been converted over the years to what could be likened to Lord Nelson's ship. His jeweller's attention to detail showed everywhere, from leather straps securing items in multiple hide holes, to sliding brass latches which closed to lock drawers in place.

Initial preparations before leaving on this journey included the setting up of a fundraiser to be attached to the ride. I love kids, and, as well as my adult art classes, I continue to teach children's drawing classes in my studio at home. Over the years I have taught some children with varying health issues.

The Royal Children's Hospital and the Starlight Foundation would benefit from any money I could raise along the way. I organised it through the recognised 'everydayhero' website, where donations could be made.

Through the website, and having stuck posters in the back windows of Frank's van, people were to give over seven hundred dollars.

Having sorted out the packing of his van the week before, Frank arrived with my bike on the back, covered over with a floral, fringed bedspread and tied with rope. Oh God, what was I thinking? We set off with me looking back at Em, and her looking at me.

I quickly decided this could possibly be a big mistake. Frank's driving was terrifying. He'd sail through red lights, over double

The World is Your Pearl

lines, out in front of speeding vehicles, do U-turns with cars bearing down on us, and brake suddenly, making snap decisions. He drove as if he was invincible. There were many times when I covered my face in terror, and he would calmly say, "No problems." The van had a hand throttle which he used for cruise control, and there was a governor on the engine, so top speed at a rattle was 88.5 kph.

As I continued with Frank in the van, the terror lasted three days as we drove to Horsham for the first night, on to Glenelg for the second, and, terror of terrors, through Adelaide before we were spat out on the other side towards Port Augusta. This had already been some journey.

In courtesy, Frank had a habit of driving right over inside the bridle of the road to allow faster vehicles to pass. At one point while driving towards Glenelg, we were driving almost in the gravel along the highway, with Frank's foot flat to the floor, when a huge transport passed us.

Frank had nowhere to go with no time to slow down as we hurtled towards the pylon of a bridge. I couldn't speak. All the blood drained from my face as the transport driver planted his foot to get past just in the nick of time. When we arrived at the caravan park that night, I said, "Sorry, Frank, but if you don't stay on the road, inside the white line, I'm bailing in Adelaide." He agreed.

Frank was a dear soul, and did his best while driving through the unfamiliar busy traffic of Adelaide. I was glad to get out of the city the next day and into open country. After staying the night in Port Augusta, my Nullarbor ride started the following morning.

Port Augusta

People asked if I'd trained for it. I hadn't, but I got my training on the job. Starting off with 68 kilometres the first day, each day varied, working up to a daily average of 100 kilometres, depending on hills and headwinds. The longest day was 130.28 kilometres. In six weeks (over 44 days) I took nine rest days.

From the first day of riding I slowly started to settle. I was a wreck when I parted company with Emma in Daylesford on the first day, dubious about how I was going to tolerate being in close proximity with one person for six weeks. Frank's driving was still a little scary but out on the open road we both started to relax. Frank waved to every driver. We began to settle into a way of easy living, with no fuss. Frank locked the bike and covered it every night. We both woke before dawn each morning.

The van had a permanent bed at one end where Frank slept, and mine was converted each night from the dining table which folded under, and cushions slid over to make up a very comfortable arrangement. We stayed in caravan parks or camped at roadhouses with amenities. In the mornings, I went off to the showers. By the time I returned, Frank had the bed packed up and the table set for breakfast. I would eat, then offer to wash up, only to be told, "No, off you go, lassie, I've got all morning to do the clean-up". I was very spoilt. I rode from around 8:00 a.m. until sunset every day with stops for a cuppa and lunch along the way. As the sun went down, Frank found me along the road and we'd head for the next roadhouse for a meal and to stay the night.

And so it went for six weeks in the rhythm of Forrest Gump, not running, but riding out of the heartbreak of the loss of my brother, and turning it into a positive experience. I had 12,000 songs on my iPod and a beautiful set of Sennheiser headphones which Emma bought for me as a Mother's Day/going away present. The cycling began to unravel my mind in a meditation and helped me to regain

The World is Your Pearl

Riding the Nullarbor – 2010

a new perspective on life. My body and mind became content to a point where things could be seen afresh and seemed to click into place. As I rode with the music on 'shuffle' I blew away a lot of cobwebs while Frank watched a lot of ants!

Early mornings on the bike were utterly magnificent with the sun on my back, listening to the superb sound of my music; I was in heaven riding into the crisp air. The scenery was constant red earth, scattered with scrubby bush as I rode for hours at a time. The road train drivers were really good and mostly gave me a very wide berth. The oncoming road trains caused more side-wind than those that passed right next to me. Lots of people hooted or flashed their lights and waved. I kept a journal of my ride.

Doing the Forrest Gump Across the Nullarbor ~ 2010 ~

Kimba

In the distance, a dot coming towards me between Kimba and Poochera, was a guy called Leigh. We both stopped to chat. He was walking from Perth to Brisbane, pushing a trailer, which fluttered with his undies hanging out to dry. It was stacked with a heavy canvas tent, a solar panel and all his survival gear. His routine was to get up at 4:00 a.m. and walk for ten hours till 2:00 p.m. He wanted to get as far as he could over the next three months before uni started. He was slathered in sunscreen and a dirty white long-sleeved t-shirt, and had dreadlocks, beautiful teeth and a handsome face. He was pretty gorgeous. Everyone was just great to talk to, and there was a respect for each other out there.

It was the same with roadhouse staff, truck drivers and travellers alike. All relaxed, laid-back, friendly, with nothing to prove. We were all just 'there'.

My dreams were bizarre. One night I dreamt a strange man was robbing my house. I was surprised to see he had missed a stack of $100 bills on the window sill. He glared back at me with a monkey grimace and left on a funny little yellow tricycle with a matching yellow trailer.

I woke fresh, and commenced the day's ride of 71.66 kilometres, which was only a little more than that of the previous one. My left knee was wincing with lots of uphill riding, and the headwinds were enough to slow me down to nine kilometres an hour at times. My top speed was only 40 kph.

Poochera

Frank and I stopped at Poochera to look at a hut made of pressed kerosene tins. A sign out the front said it was 'Peter's Humpy'. Peter had been a reclusive bachelor who worked as a stockman and station hand. The floor was compacted hard dirt with mats made from wheat bags. The bunk bed, cupboards, table and chair were made from kerosene boxes. He died aged 83 from cancer of the lip from chewing tobacco.

Frank told me the story of fifty years ago when he and Shirley travelled around on holiday in the van. They picked up a hitchhiker who was walking from farm to farm offering his services as a wheat bag sewer. He hand mended the bags for the wheat farmers. These were hard times. He was about sixteen years old, and one of seventeen kids, all working to save up to buy their mum and dad a car.

As Frank was telling me this, I recalled hearing my father telling me that my great-great-grandfather, once a drover, mended wheat bags to make ends meet later in his life.

Wirulla
We stopped for a coffee at the general store at Wirrulla. Sitting out the front was a man and his little four-year-old daughter Isla. She was covered in dirt and green ice cream. They were waiting for her eight-year-old brother Ryan to get off the bus from school. Their father was a single dad bringing them up alone in this remote town. He did odd jobs including maintaining the football ground. He couldn't find a babysitter so little Isla had to ride on the front of the motor mower. We chatted to them for a while until the school bus came.

Ceduna
Back on the bike, I rode in glorious sunshine as we continued on to Ceduna, a town on the Great Southern Ocean. Frank pulled in to a lovely caravan park by the bay. We ate dinner that evening next to a very drunk couple. The woman had been smashed up in several car accidents over her lifetime.

I was glad to stay here the next day for a no-ride day as we continued to rest in Ceduna. It was a quiet, suburban seaside town

Doing the Forrest Gump Across the Nullarbor ~ 2010 ~

with strip shops on either side of the main street. In the centre of town was the Ceduna pub. I went in to find internet coverage to contact the folks back home.

It was 10:00 a.m. Pub opening time. And some young Indigenous women came in with their children. I asked one girl if I could photograph her little child for my Fairy Green series of paintings of Wurundjeri fairies which I was hoping to include in some children's fairy books I was producing. I was suddenly surrounded by a dozen families wanting their children photographed to be in the 'fairy book'.

Watercolour sketches for Wurundjeri Fairies

My body was tired and I felt strung out from several days on the bike. Frank connected with a few people in the caravan park, and I walked out to the end of the jetty after lunch and sat there alone in a long meditation for several hours. The water was as calm as a sheet of glass. People came and went to go fishing or just to stroll. In the pub that night, the place was packed. Frank and I had a nice meal, chatted to a few of the locals and watched the entertainment. There was a spinning wheel and we bought tickets for a chook raffle, which included other prizes. I won a dozen bottles of red wine, which Frank and I enjoyed each evening wherever we camped along the way.

In the shower block the next morning I trimmed my hair with a razor. I stopped to talk to a lady who asked about my ride. She had just seen a group of blind cyclists riding towards Melbourne from Perth. They were escorted by assistants for their journey. It made me feel grateful for the thousandth time of how fortunate I was to have vision and the physical abilities to be able to do the things I did.

Nullarbor
Riding towards the Nullarbor Roadhouse, I met up with Frank and we walked out to a whale-watching platform, but there were no whales on the day we were there. By the time we came back this way in June it would be the birthing season.

Doing the Forrest Gump Across the Nullarbor ~ 2010 ~

I ran into some cyclists from Bribie Island in Queensland. They were a group of four men, one of them was a cancer survivor. They were riding from Norseman to Ceduna to celebrate his survival. Now, they laughingly joked that they wished he'd died. Luckily for them, as we parted in opposite directions, they got the tail wind. I got the head wind. They told me the road shoulder would widen after the South Australia/Western Australian border, but that it would be pretty narrow the next day. Only six inches wide.

Frank enjoyed this adventure in a very different way than me on my bike. It was surprising how many people there were for him to talk to as he stopped here and there throughout each day. He would travel along, quite separately to me. It would have been difficult having him sitting on my wheel the whole way, and quite boring and limiting for him too. We operated happily, in an easy pattern. Our routine was to meet up somewhere along the roadside each day for morning tea and lunch. At other times he would stop randomly somewhere to wait for me if we hadn't seen each other for several hours.

Every evening before dusk, Frank would pick me up and put my bike on the back of the van, then together we'd head for the next roadhouse for a meal and to camp the night. I became stronger with my riding every day, and fell into a deep, restorative sleep each night. There was never any point where I felt lonely or scared during my rides. In fact, it was quite the opposite. With the diverse range of music on my iPod, it included a lot of traditional Aboriginal music, which, although I had no Aboriginal heritage, somehow connected me spiritually to this vast Australian land.

Tonight, the sky was spectacular with fizzing sheet lightning of red/orange streaks which caused an orange blaze as it lit up the atmosphere at the base. By the time we arrived at the Nullarbor Roadhouse to camp for the night, people were staring into the sky and taking photos of the spectacular phenomenon of the Aurora Australis.

The sky was blazing with a miracle of magenta pink magnetic particles, not into the sunset, but backwards, south-east towards Tasmania.

I found out that this aurora is created by the excitation of very fast-moving electrons striking oxygen and nitrogen atoms in the upper atmosphere as the plasma ejected by the sun travels along our planet's magnetic field lines towards the North and South Poles.

Because the shockwaves sent out by the sun were so large, they easily covered the Earth's entire magnetic field, meaning an aurora appeared at both poles at the same time. At the South Pole, it was called Aurora Australis, while in the North the phenomenon was termed Aurora Borealis.

Mundrabilla

One week in, and I was just starting to adjust to the different pace of life. Frank and I were into a good routine. The four cyclists were leaving to head east at the same time I was walking out with my bike. The windsock was pointing to the ground. I rode along for just over 26 kilometres into a headwind, to a point where I met up again with Frank and we left the highway to look at the magnificent Great Australian Bight. The colour of the sea was turquoise and a variety of spectacular blues. It was a breathtaking sight beyond the jagged, cavernous cliffs which dropped to ninety feet below.

As I rode out after lunch the landscape changed to ranges on the right and shrubbery on the left which caused the headwind to disappear.

Just as I was about to get back on the bike, there was another dot behind me in the distance. It was a cyclist, going my way. We stopped to chat for a few minutes to introduce ourselves. His name was Erden Eruc. As we rode together along the Eyre Highway for 80 kilometres over the next few hours, I learned his amazing story.

Doing the Forrest Gump Across the Nullarbor ~ 2010 ~

Erden Eruc – Follow his journeys:- www.around-n-over.org

He was born in Cyprus, and raised in Turkey. He came from Seattle, USA, and was pulling a heavy rig with a solar panel, satellite phone, laptop, tent, water, food, stove and fuel. Pretty much everything he required for a full life on the road.

Having reached Australia in February, he'd ridden 6,300 kilometres from Cooktown to the point where we met up in June. But his journey started three years prior, in July 2007. He was circumnavigating the earth entirely by human power. By the time he came up beside me on my bike, he'd covered around 28,000 kilometres. Whilst doing this, he was conquering the highest summit on each continent he touched. So far he had climbed Mount McKinley in Alaska and Mount Kosciuszko, Australia. Mount Kilimanjaro in Africa was next. Aconcagua, Elbrus and Everest were also on his list. These summits were in memory of his close mate, Göran Kropp, whom he had lost when they'd been rock climbing together.

The World is Your Pearl

Göran owned an adventure company and was famous for his bicycle ride in 1996 towing his climbing gear behind him on a trailer from Stockholm in Sweden to Nepal to climb Everest without porter assistance.

Erden and Göran had been on a short climb together in September 2002 in Eastern Washington State in the United States. When Göran took a fall from a height of about 20 metres, his protection failed and he hit the ledge Erden was on and died. His body had to be lifted out by helicopter.

When the accident happened, Göran's rope had wrapped around Erden's arm, causing him to suffer severe muscle strangulation of his left triceps muscle. As he described this, Erden pointed to his sleeve. I felt it. A terrible injury. His arm looked like the twist in a sausage.

His decision to circumnavigate the earth was in honour of Göran and to raise funds for his own nonprofit organisation called Around-n-Over to educate and inspire mainly children. He supported boarding students in primary schools in rural Turkey and especially young girls who didn't otherwise have the opportunity to have an education.

Before he began his circumnavigation by human power, he spent 96 days at sea in a rowboat from the Canary Islands to Guadeloupe from January to May 2006 to prove to sponsors that he was serious and ready for the crossing of the Pacific Ocean. The primary sponsor AKTAS Holding, makers of rubber automotive suspension units, was impressed with his focus, stamina and abilities.

By the time Erden met up with his sponsor, he'd covered 8,500 kilometres, cycling from Seattle to Alaska, then pulled a sled across glaciers to reach the foothills of Mt McKinley. As we rode together across the Nullarbor, he described that journey. By the time he came off the mountain all the snow was melting and the blossoms were in bloom.

He married his fiancée, Nancy, in a Native American ceremony in a fjord across from Homer, Alaska. But there was no honeymoon. Nancy flew home and he got back on his bicycle. As he cycled back across Alaska and Yukon, brown bears and black bears were on the roads, having come out of hibernation.

He arrived at the top of Australia from Papua New Guinea, where he'd walked the island north to south using the Kokoda Track then rowed for 33 days from Port Moresby to the tip of Cape York. He then used a sea kayak to reach Cooktown before riding down the east coast of Australia to reach Kosciuszko. Then pedalled west across the Nullarbor to the desolate point where we'd met up and ridden along together.

Mundrabilla

Frank met up with us here and there along the way. It was getting dark and beginning to rain as we all eventually stopped at Mundrabilla, renowned to be the place where a meteorite landed in 1911. Its composition was mostly iron and nickel, and it weighed 22 tonnes.

The three of us enjoyed a meal together. The food at every roadhouse was hearty and home-cooked by country chefs. The meal tonight was no exception. I ordered hot pea and ham soup, and a chicken, bacon and mushroom casserole with crispy roasted potatoes, pumpkin and peas. Over more cups of tea we chatted a while longer before Erden had to head off to write for his book, on his laptop. He stayed in one of the roadhouse accommodation rooms, and we camped for the night.

I have stayed in contact with Erden to the present day. By the end of his journey on July 21, 2012, he had covered a total distance of 66,299 kilometres. Throughout his travels, he maintained a website called www.around-n-over.org where he kept a meticulous blog and regularly held conference calls with little school kids in Turkey via a satellite phone. They waited for his calls from wherever he was in the world.

Cocklebiddy

The following morning, after cups of tea and another long chat we said goodbye to Erden, and I left to ride to Cocklebiddy. Today's ride was only 58.34 kilometres.

Erden Eruc with Glenda Wise

The Nullarbor was well named. In Latin it means no trees. Nullus=nothing. Arbor=tree.

It has the longest straight road on the planet, which runs in one continuous section for 146.6 kilometres from Caiguna to Balladonia.

There were beautiful riding conditions all day. So far I had seen no wildlife to speak of. I rode past a field mouse licking a very tiny roadkill, one small lone kangaroo and two wedge-tailed eagles, but apart from a few crows eating lots of dead things, it was utterly remarkable to see nothing.

Balladonia

I met five guys cycling from Perth to Adelaide. They flew over to Perth to ride back. Their trailers were great little set-ups. They had water dropped to them all the way, and gave us 40 litres they couldn't use. They were fundraising for the Children's Heart Foundation and, like me, they had an everydayhero website for their fundraiser. Theirs was called *Tour de heart 2010 for kids*.

Tour de heart riders

Further down the road there was another dot. It was a man walking from Perth to Sydney pushing a wheelchair with a life-sized brown teddy bear dressed in clothes. He was raising awareness and gathering funds for the disabled.

Today's ride was 100.7 kilometres to Balladonia. The skies at night were like black velvet, sandblasted with the stars of the Milky Way. This myriad of twinklers formed a dome to the horizon.

Norseman

It was hard to believe I had only been riding for a week since commencing my ride from Port Augusta. It was now May 18. Today's ride was 101.37 kilometres, and took seven hours over lots of hills. Once I'd done the ride I got into the van to travel with Frank and the roads were downhill or flat for the rest of the way to Norseman.

Lots of nutty things went on in the desert. People amused themselves along the way by tying little bushes up with ribbon. I'd seen them for hundreds of kilometres. Others dressed up rocks with clothes, hats and sunglasses, with sticks for arms. There were large, mostly dead, trees decorated with one thing. One of them was covered with shoes, another with bras. Another had bottles hanging from strings, another with undies. They were three or four hundred kilometres apart, and must have been added to over many years.

As I washed some clothes in the laundry of the Norseman Caravan Park, I met a couple from Pakenham in Victoria who were great friends of Jack Montgomery, a friend of Dad's from my childhood. It didn't matter where I went on earth, there were six degrees of separation.

Esperance

The following day I rode 109.06 kilometres to Esperance. Heading out on the bike that morning, the riding started out easy, followed by a 30 kilometre uphill, then some great downhills. It was a brilliant

Doing the Forrest Gump Across the Nullarbor ~ 2010 ~

day and we were now travelling south. The sun was on my back and the light was different, as was the landscape and vegetation. I rode past unusual salmon gum trees with trunks like burnished copper and bronze.

Remarkably, so far, the weather had been clear and sunny by day, and cold to freezing by night. Some nights were so cold, Frank would place a sheet of cardboard on the large window at the back of the van where he slept. On occasional mornings there was ice on the bike cover. It seemed to me that all things were *sorted* the whole way, as if by some higher source. The only time the weather turned bad coincided with the times when there was no way of riding due to the road conditions being too narrow, with steep gravel drop-offs to the side and nowhere to get out of the way of passing trucks.

Even the condition of the bike was sorted. Before leaving on this journey, my cycling coach, Peter Warren, loaned me two spare wheels and sent me off with ten new tyre tubes. But I didn't pump the tyres once for the duration of the trip.

There was only one glitch which must surely have happened for a reason, where, this time, it was me who was sorted.

Riding down from Norseman to Esperance, I ran out of daylight. I had no light on my bike as there was never the intention to ride in the dark. But in the west, there seemed to be no dusk, and the day went to dark quite suddenly by 5:00 p.m.

I was in strife as Frank had gone ahead into Esperance. I clipped a flashing light onto the back of my helmet as the road got narrower. Eventually I couldn't see enough to watch the condition of the road surface. I picked up the bike and started walking, when suddenly the back wheel fell off. By then it was really dark. I put the bike over my shoulder and picked up the wheel and held it up to the first set of headlights I saw coming behind me.

The World is Your Pearl

A huge, burly guy called Shaun, driving a 4WD, did a U-turn and picked me up. He ran the Caltex fuel depot which supplied all the massive farm equipment throughout the Mallee district. He put the bike on top of his pile of wood in the back and drove me ten kilometres into Esperance. Dear old Frank was stationed in full view of the crossroads as we came in. He'd waited an hour with only moths to watch (no ants) ...

I was exhausted by the time we found a meal at the pub in Esperance that night. As we walked past the bare-breasted barmaid in the topless bar to get to the dining room, it crossed my mind that those perky nipples were totally wasted on us. There were a few guys in there who were fascinated to talk to us.

One road worker was keen to tell me how many cyclists he'd scraped off the highways who'd been hit by road trains. "Basically nothing left." His mate Damian was awestruck and said, "You're a legend" and wished he was doing it with me. He loved bikes with a passion, and while the negative guy was talking he was shaking his head and giving me the thumbs up. He worked for the biggest bike importer in Perth and knew all about my brand of road racing bike, the Hasa. He said he'd be honoured to service it, so I was glad for him to put my wheel back on. He went all over the bike out in the car park, then hopped on to give it a test ride and raved, saying, "This is a beautiful bike!"

His negative roadworker mate came out to continue his description of the plight of cyclists across the Nullarbor. He said, "One road train hit a cyclist and didn't even know it till he was hosing the truck down a day later when bike and bits of mashed person dropped out." He said he'd seen some amazing things. He saw an Asian guy walking from Perth to Melbourne pushing a wheelie bin which he slept in at night!

It was lovely to have a rest day in Esperance. I had a sleep-in and we sat for ages over breakfast. It was a warm, sunny day in a lovely old established seaside caravan park. Later, while we ate our lunch, Frank said, "I always think sea is more interesting than mountain. There's nice movement by the sea, much more of interest to look at, watching the waves coming in."

I chatted to several groups of people. The couple camped in front of us were Jill and David Burke from Bairnsdale in Victoria, who knew Frank's best mate Bertie Lamshed's daughter. The guy camped beside us was Mark. He had a huge Triumph motorbike and a base station mobile home, and came from Emerald, a town only a few kilometres from where I lived. He was born in the William Angliss Bush Hospital where my father, my brother, I and both my children were born, and he went to the Ferntree Gully Technical School where my brother attended as a boy 42 years ago.

It was now the 13th day of 44 days riding. Before we left this morning, campers Jill and David Burke called around to say there was a huge weather front coming through and gave me $50 for the Starlight Foundation. Other people came around to tell us there was a big low coming across, with stormy weather predicted for Saturday and Sunday.

Frank and I enjoyed the rest in Esperance very much. It was a beautiful seaside town with a little market in the community square, nice shops and a happy holiday feel. The weather had been glorious as we wandered around. After picking up some provisions, we set out again. I got on the bike and we headed for Ravensthorpe. I could only ride 71.74 kilometres before the road disintegrated to become narrow, with steep gravel drop-offs. Sure enough, this coincided with the approach of the bad weather. It was perfect timing and, after having driven my body for so long, I was glad of the rest.

Albany

I became a passenger for a couple of days as we drove through the vast wheat-growing area of Mallee country between the Esperance Plains and the Avon wheat belt. We continued on through the Coolgardie Region and the Stirling Ranges to Albany. By this time the weather had turned so violent, we were nearly blown off the face of the earth!

This was a terrible stretch of road. It was narrow and dangerous in very bad condition with rough, soft edges. There were no roadsides, just steep gravel drop-offs. The double lines continued for so many miles that if someone had a flat tyre, there would be no way of pulling off the road, nor for other vehicles to pass.

Frank thought the roads were a disgrace. He couldn't understand why Western Australia didn't have their A1 highway in better repair. He explained that the coal industry in Queensland subsidises their roads. Western Australia, with its billions of dollars in wealth coming from its huge industries like gold, gas, iron ore, wheat, cattle, sheep, copper, fishing and tourism could easily afford it. Yet, he said, a lot of this money ends up overseas. It appeared to be no better than a fourth-rate country road in Victoria.

There was no letup in the weather for two days. We camped the night in Albany. The wind roared for hours, rocking the van wildly, and heavy torrential rain pelted so much it was hard to sleep.

Manjimup

This was a hellish time. Frank did his best, but his driving was horrendous as we flew along, speeding in the wet. It was terrifying. I couldn't wait to stop. Once again, my wish came true when suddenly the windscreen wipers pegged out 40 kilometres from Manjimup. We had to pull over to wait for the rain to ease enough for Frank to fix them.

Doing the Forrest Gump Across the Nullarbor ~ 2010 ~

In the shower block where we camped for the night at Manjimup were huge Bogong and Cossid moths. Some were as big as a man's hand. Frank's knowledge was remarkable. He told me they once formed an important food source for the Aborigines. Crushed moths and their larvae were equivalent to butter fat, so necessary in their diet. The moths' larvae provided a delicious snack when lightly roasted. The taste was reputed to be like cream cheese, their skin like pork crackling.

Perth

This epic Nullarbor journey is more suitable for a book than a chapter, so can't be fully described here. However, one of the highlights for Frank on this trip was a visit to the Royal Perth Yacht Club. As a young man, he joined the army and was in the Second/Third Anti-Aircraft Battalion. They used Bofors guns and he spent five years in the military forces in the Middle East, Papua New Guinea, Colombo, Suez Canal, Tobruk and Java. Then he was sent to Broome and Perth in Western Australia.

Frank was lucky during his war service in that he saw very little serious combat. Most of his postings were to protect bases from air attack that rarely came. When asked what they did in Perth, he replied, "Protecting Perth from Japanese attack." The questioner said, "But the Japanese never attacked Perth." Frank said, "We did a good job, didn't we?"

The site of the Royal Perth Yacht Club was in Crawley, on Pelican Point where Frank's gun emplacement once stood in 1942. I walked with him out along the jetty where he pointed to the spot where the American speed boats were once tethered. They took their pilots out to the Catalina seaplanes, which flew from this spot to Timor and back in one day.

Frank had brought along a beautiful set of large black-and-white photographs of this spot as it was in 1942. The general manager and the commodore of the yacht club greeted Frank warmly and were fascinated to talk to him. They arranged for scans of his photos to be made, and treated us to lunch in the formal dining room upstairs.

Cunderin

Devastation struck in a small way this morning. As Frank was moving my bike, he accidentally zeroed out my trip meter. Luckily I had photographed my most recent 1000 kilometres on the odometer and had diligently noted all ride distances in my journal each day.

As I rode out of the Cunderdin Caravan Park at 8:30 a.m., the day was clear and sunny. We had passed what seemed like millions of acres of wheat fields throughout Western Australia. Today I rode along parallel to the big Perth-Kalgoorlie water pipeline, and the rail line. Frank told me the sad story of the engineer responsible for the water pipe to Kalgoorlie. He was ridiculed so much when it was thought not to have been successful that he committed suicide. Two weeks later, the water flowed through.

I had ridden along for two hours, when who should I run into coming the other way, but Erden. Frank saw him too, and turned around to come back to greet him with a handshake and Erden gave me a hug and a kiss.

When we'd turned south to Esperance, Erden had travelled north to Kalgoorlie.

Frank invited him to join us for an early lunch of biscuits and cheese, some fruit and a coffee. Erden told us that by the time he would reach Perth he'd have missed the tide. The boat he had ready for the next leg of his human-powered journey would be shrink-wrapped and put into storage. Instead, he would continue to ride on to Geraldton. From there he would need to do a turnaround back to Seattle for visa purposes, so would dismantle the bike and trailer and have them packed up and sent on too.

With a promise to catch up when he and his new wife Nancy were back in Australia, we parted in opposite directions. My day's ride was a record distance of 131.69 kilometres, making a total so far of 1168.69 kilometres. I ended my ride at dusk, and got off the bike as a huge flock of red-tailed black cockatoos took flight.

Burracoppin

The town where I stopped and met up with Frank was Burracoppin. Way too primitive to stay in, according to Frank. He'd sussed it out. The camp had no hot water and the pub was closed for a private party. With the bike on the back of the van, we travelled on in the dark for a further 66 kilometres to Southern Cross.

After settling into the caravan park, we crossed the road for a magnificent dinner in the Palace Hotel. They had a roaring fire and there were people everywhere at the bar and in the dining area. One group of eight people had known each other since they were little kids and camp holidayed every year. Over bottles of red wine with their dinner, they were playing the jukebox and having a ball.

Southern Cross

There was a lady travelling alone in a small camper van. She sat outside in the morning sun at a folding table with a lace tablecloth and a small flowerpot. She was eating her breakfast over a pot of tea while reading a book. I loved this transient lifestyle. The scene made me think how nice it would be to declutter, and just drift along, doing this on a permanent basis.

For a person who was happy with their own company, there would never be a chance to feel lonely. Stopping at the end of each day there was always someone to talk to. We'd seen her chatting to some travellers in the dining room of the pub the night before.

True to Erden's warnings, the road as we left Southern Cross became pretty bad with rough edges, so I rode for a while with

Frank towards Coolgardie. It wasn't long before I got back on the bike. The road conditions varied but the tankers and road trains continued to go around me. I rode for approximately 8.5 hours for 104 kilometres over quite a few hills. Dinner tonight was bully beef and baked beans. I slept like a log.

Coolgardie

Staying in Coolgardie, there was a prospector and his wife camped next to us. They were from Sale in Victoria. They went on prospecting tours each year with 20 caravans or more into private land areas. One guy found nuggets weighing 80 oz in two weeks. Nuggets are far more valuable than refined gold.

They had a son and daughter living in Narre Warren and Endeavour Hills, close to where I live.

Their son was a road train driver. In 2010, his wages were $130,000 per annum. He worked two weeks on and one week off. After a minimum of six months, his airfares were paid to wherever he wanted to go in Australia.

They explained that the road trains never stopped. They were driven 600 kilometres a day as the drivers exchanged shifts. Drivers received a fitness regime from instructors every morning, breakfasts in the mess hall, and a choice of lunch box to take with them. Their wages were around $2400 per week. Those working on Barrow Island off Karratha earned $3000 per week as this was an indigenous dry area. Unlike the wild situation I'd seen in Bougainville, each driver was drug and alcohol tested every morning.

They told us stories about events and people in the outback, and said it wasn't about the gold to be found. The gold was in the people they'd met along the way.

Doing the Forrest Gump Across the Nullarbor ~ 2010 ~

Kalgoorlie

Another great highlight of the trip was a tour of the Kalgoorlie Gold Mine. For $60 each, it was money well spent as we were driven through the massive Super Pit of the open cut mine site for two hours. This was the second largest gold mine in the world. The largest was in South Africa. We were taken around in an enclosed 12-person vehicle as an official mine worker described the operations of the mine.

When we were there in 2010, the size of the pit was 1706 feet deep, and yielded 20 tons of gold per year. Its tunnels were 3.5 kilometres long, and 1640 feet wide, and went down 5250 feet. If placed end to end, the early (pick and shovel) tunnels measured 4500 kilometres.

He told us that by the year 2021 their lease would be up. At that point, unless they were still commanding great gold prices, the huge pit would be filled with water. Due to its sheer size, this would take 30 years. However there was still another 100 years of ore to be had. The scale and depth of the mine was awe-inspiring, and the capacity of every bit of machinery associated with the mining process was gigantic, and valued at many millions of dollars.

I can't help but list a few of the many facts and figures described to us as we moved around the site at a safe distance from its massive machinery.

- All mine workers were required to live in Kalgoorlie as there were no fly in fly outs.
- 8000 tons of rock went through the crusher every day.
- Male and female Caterpillar drivers earned $100,000.00 per year. (in 2010)
- Face Shovel drivers earned $125,000.00 per year.
- The train drivers out of Newman and Tom Price received $180,000.00 per year. (Train drivers, we were told, had boring jobs.)

The World is Your Pearl

- The trains of 200 wagons filled with ore were 7.25 kilometres long, weighed 100,000 tons, and were pushed by seven locomotives.
- The dump trucks were valued at 3.5 million dollars each, and ran continuously day and night using 200 litres of diesel fuel per hour, and could carry up to 256 tons.
- The face shovels weighed 700 tons, so could only move 2 kilometres an hour. They picked up 70 tons of rock soil in each scoop, four scoops for each truck. The weight of each scoop was automatically measured.
- Throughout the mine, 450 tons of rock or waste was moved per hour.
- Salt water was used to wet the roads of the site to keep the dust down.
- The 20 tons of gold extracted each year was 90% pure.
- Each tier of the pit was 98 feet to the next.
- Drivers swapped and changed for variation of jobs. This was called 'hot seating'.

We'd loved the rest day in Kalgoorlie with its history of mining and Chinese joss houses, and went up one last time to have a look at the Super Pit from the public viewing platform above, before we left.

The narrow road from Kalgoorlie was treacherous with red dirt edges which were soft and stony. I had only ridden for 30 seconds when a road train with four trailers went past on the other side of the road. The wind blast from its weight rocked my bike. Two passing in opposite directions would have been disastrous. I had no choice but to abandon my riding and drive with Frank to Norseman. We ate lunch in the picnic ground. From here it was only a half-day ride of 68 kilometres.

Frazer Range

Two of my dear friends, Joan and Mick, often ride motorcycles around Australia. Before I left Melbourne, they told me the Frazer Range Sheep Station was not to be missed. It was beautiful. As I walked up the hill behind the station there was a vast scene of plains in every direction. It was 437,000 acres,(160 kilometres) from north to south, which allowed one sheep per 27 acres. This minimised erosion and overgrazing. We were told this station was small compared to the 600,000 acre property next to it. They were once one station of 1,000,037 acres. The property was beautifully appointed with big shearing sheds, ranch house accommodations, hot showers and kitchens.

In the evening we sat on smooth split logs by a roaring campfire chatting to some other campers. One was a lady who'd seen us in another camp. She gave us $30 for the Royal Children's Hospital. She had been a midwife but had given it away as she couldn't cope with the babies dying. She moved to the children's burns section, which she said was like going from the frying pan to the pot.

Balladonia

June 4 was a special day. Frank drove me out to the highway to begin my road ride and returned to join the station caretakers for coffee and a long chat. A couple of hours later he waved to me as he passed. It was lovely weather, though a slow day today with lots of hills and headwinds. As I was riding slowly up a long hill after lunch, I could see the red dot of Frank's van in the distance.

As I came closer, there were the flashing lights of a police car and two gorgeous, very tall, young policewomen talking to him. I pulled over and said, "What have you done *now*, Frank?" He looked at the girls, while looking down and kicking a stone with his foot, and said, "Don't be too hard on me, officers, it's my 91st birthday." Frank was born on 4th June 1919.

The World is Your Pearl

"Just a routine licence check," they chuckled, more curious than anything. Frank showed them around the inside of the van while they chatted. They could hardly get through the door with all their guns and walkie talkies. One of them was Emma. She asked if we were doing the ride for charity.

They put their hands in their pockets and pulled out their lunch money to put in the donation box. I took photos of them for Frank's birthday shot.

Frank's 91st birthday

He'd had a lovely time this morning as he hadn't expected anyone to know. At breakfast, Frank shed a tear as I gave him a wrapped gift of a dark-green, fine wool vest, a wood carving and a card. And the people at Fraser Station presented him with a peaked cap, with Fraser Station embroidered on it.

Cocklebiddy

There were other people doing various solo stints. I met up with them hundreds of kilometres from anywhere, two little dots in the opposite distance as we came closer and closer to each other. One was Deborah de Williams. We stopped to talk on the vast empty highway between Balladonia and Cocklebiddy, on the Nullarbor Plain. She was on foot, running 18,026 kilometres around Australia to raise funds for breast cancer research. So far she had raised a remarkable $140,000.00! We gave each other a donation. Megan Norris wrote a book about her journey called *Running Pink*. I was told years later that she mentioned Frank and I within its pages, describing me as his wife!

The World is Your Pearl

Meeting Deborah De Williams 'Running Pink'

Eucla

On the ground, all along the roadside around Eucla, were millions of what Frank thought seemed like tiny thunder eggs, or meteorites. We stopped to fossick for a while together, gathering lots of these perfectly round little stones. I found out they were nodules, formed in the soil overlying the limestone of the Eucla Basin. They were around two million years old, each one formed by the layer-by-layer build-up of calcium carbonate, around a grain of lime.

Doing the Forrest Gump Across the Nullarbor ~ 2010 ~

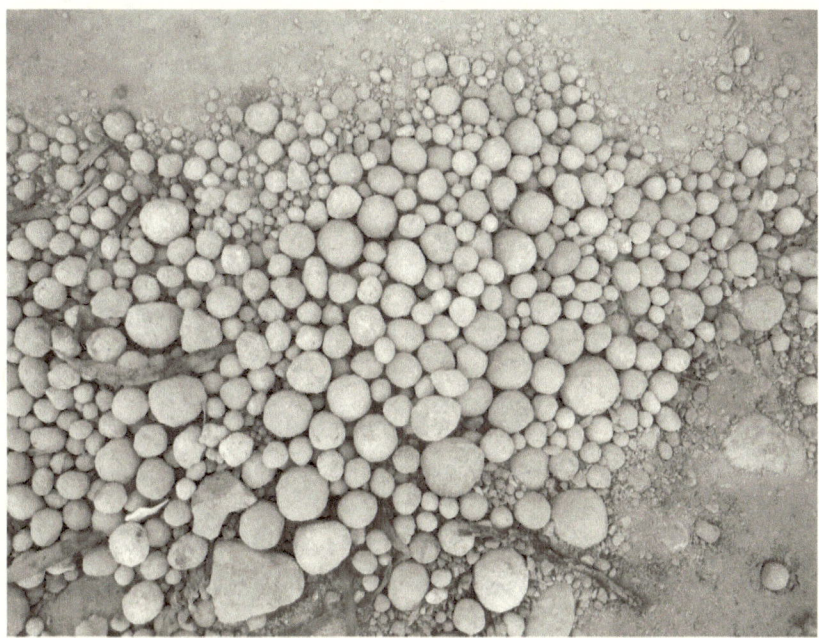

The Nullarbor itself is a dry, flat, 200,000 square kilometre savannah, stretching 1100 kilometres along the southern coast of Australia from Balladonia, east of Norseman, Western Australia, to north of Yatala in South Australia.

Little did I know, as I rode along its desert surface, that underneath me were vast underground lakes, suspended within a karst labyrinth of the largest piece of limestone on earth, tens of millions of years old.

Aboveground it was mainly featureless. Some called it *'Nullarboring'* as it was barren, and there was little to see except for the occasional scrub of bluebush, saltbush and mulga. However, beneath the surface was a complex world of ancient underground caverns, filled with stalactites and stalagmites.

Tunnels and chambers, riddled with sinkholes like Swiss cheese, were dissolved out of rock over millions of years, by the sitting water of pristine underground lakes across four levels.

The World is Your Pearl

The water slowly worked its way through the limestone, forming a network of dolines, leading into extensive cave systems which stretch for kilometres underground. This beautiful subterranean, water-filled world is visited by cave divers, scientists and explorers from all over the globe. The water is so crystal clear and still in parts it cannot be seen. As though floating in space, divers are simply suspended in it. The clarity of the water is such that someone swimming at a depth of 40 to 50 metres inside a sinkhole could look up and still see the clouds.

(I may well have been riding along the road in the desert, above a diver swimming beneath me.)

In other areas, the water moves and roars as it drains into the extensive network of blow holes, according to the air pressure above.

This composition of the great Nullarbor Plain explained why there was so much road-kill along the Eyre Highway. When it rains, the water falls rapidly through sand and gravel to the vast aquifer of porous limestone beneath its arid surface.

The bitumen is the main place where water pools after rain, and is where animals and eagles come to drink from puddles at the roadsides.

There are remarkable YouTube videos available via:
Journeyman Pictures: Cave-Diving in Australia's arid Nullarbor outback
ABC Science Online: The mystery of the Nullarbor caves
The University of Melbourne: Time-travelling under the Nullarbor

It had been a shorter ride today after yesterday's tough 110.47 kilometre ride through strong headwinds. I had ridden six and a half hours straight. The skies were drab as we stopped early to

Doing the Forrest Gump Across the Nullarbor ~ 2010 ~

camp at Eucla. I decided to ride back towards Mundarabilla to make up my 100 kilometres for the day.

A lady who I'd met in Kalgoorlie tooted and pulled over. She leapt out of her car and ran across to give me a hug, saying, "I can't believe you've made it all this way. We were placing bets that there was no way you'd be this far along," she said. "Can you wait? I want to give you some money." She ran back to her car and came back with a donation of $10.

As the lady drove off, I continued for eight kilometres before turning around to ride back to Eucla. A guy riding a recumbent bike came alongside. His name was Peter Heal. He'd ridden from Sydney, over the top end, down the west coast of Australia to where I met him as he was heading across the Nullarbor Plain. We chatted

Peter Heal, riding his VK2 Velokraft recumbent bike around Australia

as we rode along together. I told him I was making up my 100 kilometres for the day. His day's ride had been an impressive 300 kilometres, 'even though he was lying down on the job'! So far he'd ridden 11,360 kilometres, and had another 4000 to complete his ride around Australia. I later learned why he had no time to stop to chat. By the time he'd completed his ride, he was to set a solo distance record, covering around 15,000 kilometres. He had cycled alone around Australia in 48 days, 23 hours and 37 minutes, lowering the previous record by approximately two days.

I found Frank's van and set out for the shower block as he locked my bike up for the night. There must have been snake problems around Eucla, as there were strict signs on all the toilets to keep the doors closed at all times.

I saw some remarkable characters along the way. One man kept popping up wherever we went. He must have hitchhiked back and forth along the highway, as we kept passing him. He wore a checked shirt and a pair of baggy trousers and slippers on his feet. All he carried was a raffia bag with his belongings. I passed another hitchhiker wearing a bra and knickers and a superman cape tied around her waist. I ran into her later at a roadhouse. She was hitchhiking around Australia.

Bordertown

I almost came to grief as I was riding from Bordertown. It was just after the Western Australia/South Australia border heading east towards the Nullarbor Roadhouse. I was riding on an undulating section when the road conditions became really bad with rough edges.

I had ridden 126 kilometres, pushed along by a great tail wind the whole way, and was feeling so good I could have ridden all the way to the Nullarbor Roadhouse. But the wind turned to a wild south-westerly and the road trains rocked me badly. This section of the

Doing the Forrest Gump Across the Nullarbor ~ 2010 ~

road was a shocker. The skies turned black, and I was thinking about packing it in, when suddenly the decision was made for me.

With the truckies' network of CB radios, there wouldn't have been a road train driver anywhere who didn't know where I was, and they'd honk from a distance to let me know they were approaching. My policy *always* was to get the bike well out of the way at all times. It was easily possible to stop and carry the bike right off the road with enough warning.

Road Train

However, on this occasion I hadn't seen the road train heading towards me as it had disappeared into a dip, and just as suddenly there was another one, right on me from behind. He didn't honk, I hadn't heard him approach, and he had another one right on his tail. There was such a steep gravel drop-off I couldn't steer away.

The World is Your Pearl

I braked so suddenly in an attempt to get the bike off the road, it went up from behind and I flew over the handlebars and landed on the bitumen. I was unhurt but badly shaken.

The road train driver slammed on his brakes and slewed sideways into the path of the oncoming one. I'm not sure how a collision was avoided, but I walked out to the front of the road train and waved to let the driver know I was still alive, but *hell, was I pissed off!* The look of relief on his face as he waved back was huge. He must have been asleep as he should have honked. For the next two days I rode with jelly legs.

Apart from Frank's driving, this was my closest encounter with death (for this trip, at least). Fortunately, the blackening skies meant that dear Frank wasn't far away, and I was grateful to travel inside the van with him in my shaken state.

Heading Home

The Nullarbor ride was a huge life event. I have only written about two-thirds of my journey here, with a further 1000 kilometres of the ride to describe. However, the places we saw and the people we met could fill a book. The stories were too numerous to fit into this chapter. I had started my ride in Port Augusta, and ridden through Iron Knob, Kimba, Poochera, Wirrulla, Ceduna, Nullarbor, Bordertown, Mundrabilla, Madura, Cocklebiddy, Caiguna, Belladonia, Norseman, down to Esperance, across to Albany, then Perth. Up to Southern Cross, Coolgardie, Kalgoorlie, returning to Norseman and back across the Nullarbor through South Australia and Victoria over a period of six weeks. I kept a meticulous log of my distances each day, took a photo of the odometer every time it clicked over another thousand kilometres and kept up with journal entries in the evenings.

The final day of the ride over a distance of 106.66 kilometres was long and hard over hills with headwinds. The road and weather

Doing the Forrest Gump Across the Nullarbor ~ 2010 ~

conditions had been so bad that my body was screaming with pain, my knee joints ached, it was getting cold and I was very fatigued. As the odometer headed towards 3000 kilometres, I continued to ride as I ran out of light approaching Shepparton, in Victoria. This was the only time I was happy for Frank to crawl along behind me to shield me from the traffic and shine his headlights on the road.

Ten kilometres before what I'd decided to round off the ride at 3000 kilometres, I pulled over. Frank stopped as I walked around to the driver's side window and said, "I've had it." Frank said, "How many?" I said, "There's another ten kilometres to go. It's over, I can't go any further." Frank looked at me and said, "Ten kilometres?" With a look of 'Are you kidding? Get on with it, girl'.

I got back on the bike with my body seizing up. Forcing myself along, I somehow rode through the pain, got my final wind, and minced and ground my way along as I watched the clicks turn over to the 3000. When I stopped, my body was completely shattered. We were in the middle of nowhere, on a road leading to Shepparton.

The sky was like indigo velvet. There was a dam in a paddock distant from the road on which a mother duck swam ahead of ducklings trailing behind her. A single huge star shone in the sky above the water, casting a ladder of light over them. As dear Frank took my bike and loaded it onto the back of the van, I looked up at the star and said, "Well, what do you think, Steve? I did it."

Amazingly, I discovered this was the shortest day of the year. It was Monday June 21, and the Winter Solstice. It was exactly two years to the day since Steve's death.

The following morning was a complete white-out. A 'pea-soup' of thick fog, so dense we had to crawl along following the white lines on the road all the way from Shepparton to Yea.

The World is Your Pearl

My dear old legendary friend had driven 7000 kilometres and we'd done the Forrest Gump together with Steve on my shoulder all the way.

I realised throughout this journey that there is no road to peace. Peace 'is' the road.

CHAPTER 9

Night Dive With the Giant Manta Rays— Hawaii ~ 2013 ~

A micro story of a BIG experience

Diving the other world.
Once the sea had cast its spell on me,
I was enraptured in its wonder forever.

I took my son Cameron and daughter Emma on a family holiday to Hawaii in 2013. They too had been born with active and adventuring spirits. Cameron was a passionate triathlete, cyclist, jet skier, and loved the sea. Emma loved snowboarding, abseiling, rock climbing, rappelling and scuba diving.

We had all attained Level Two International Dive Licences.

Emma wanted her first dive to be on Ningaloo Reef in Western Australia where her main desire was to swim with the whale sharks.

The World is Your Pearl

She flew straight to Perth and her dream came true when she encountered two of them. For her first dive, this was something she would never forget, and was to remain a pinnacle of her diving experiences. With her passion for the great creatures of the sea, one of the main things she wanted to do while in Hawaii was to go on a night dive with the giant manta rays.

We hired a Mustang convertible and Cam did all the driving. 'Cameron Troy; what a boy'. He was an ace at driving a left-hand vehicle on the other side of the road without a hitch. We had some great experiences as we moved around the islands of Hawaii, Kauai and Oahu together. With a packed agenda, in Honolulu on Oahu, we went paragliding 700 feet up in the air. Visited the zoo. Went shark diving to see a large group of Galapagos sharks. We snorkelled and went scuba diving on the reefs, where the highlight for all of us were the giant green sea turtles.

Cameron and Emma did a tandem sky dive. This triggered a passion with Cam, who has done a lot of skydiving ever since. On the Island of Kauai, we sea kayaked up the Wailau River, to hike up through lush tropical forests to the Secret (Uluwehi) Falls. We flew to the Big Island of Hawaii, hired another convertible and stayed in a lovely condo on the beach for two days.

Hawaii was quiet and much more underdeveloped than Honolulu. It was all volcanic rock, black soil, rich in minerals, and black sand beaches. We drove through tropical forests and plantations of coffee, mangos, macadamia nuts, papaya and avocado trees.

Taking a day trip, we drove to see the edge of the Kilauea Caldera in the Hawaii Volcanoes National Park. This crater opening was the size of two football fields. Silver lava and smoke constantly billowed from it. This summit caldera was the most active volcano on earth, though all quiet when we were there. However, it must have been amazing to see when a major eruption commenced. We were told

Night Dive With the Giant Manta Rays—Hawaii ~ 2013 ~

the vents roared like jet engines as they spewed forth lava and gasses under high pressure. I read that fountains of molten rock shot high into the air. The descriptions became spectacular with lava fountains, curtains of fire, lava lakes, lava cascades, spatters, cinder cones, ash blasts and steam explosions.

On the main island of Hawaii was the main thing Emma had wanted to do, and what turned out to be the biggest highlight of the trip for me. We were taken out in the late afternoon on the big *'Neptune Charlie's* boat. The waves were huge and choppy as we travelled fourteen kilometres out to sea with six other divers.

This rolling-sea trip caused Emma and I the worst sea sickness we've ever experienced. As I looked at Emma, she was visibly green, with yellow circles under her eyes, and I must have looked the same as I felt violently ill. We both felt *green around the gills*, and tried watching the horizon and sucking in the sea air in an attempt to settle down before the dive.

The big bonus of this wild sea ride as we stood on the bow was seeing a large number of tiny Spinner Dolphins, which swam alongside our boat, flipping and spinning out of the water. They put on a spectacular performance as we watched them doing full somersaults while spinning at the same time.

As the sun was setting, we arrived at the spot where the mantas congregate when they hear the sounds of the boats' motors.

There were two boats which dropped anchor and were attached to large pontoons fitted with strong spotlights which beamed down into the water. These lights attracted the bioluminescent plankton which manta rays trawled to feed on. Emma and Cameron put the scuba tanks on and went down 60 feet to the sea floor.

The World is Your Pearl

Cameron was unaffected by sea sickness, but I was really worried about how Emma would breathe if she had to throw up under water with an air reg in her mouth. Knowing just how ill she was, I'll never know how she controlled it by sheer mind strength. She had a lot of determined willpower.

Once they'd descended, I was too ill to be disappointed that I couldn't join them. In a wetsuit, fins, mask and a snorkel, I swam out to the pontoon.

This turned out to be one of the best experiences of my life. Between bouts of throwing up, I could let my stomach do all the heaving it liked while being able to breathe and look down.

The mantas started arriving. I had the full drama of these extraordinary monsters barrelling up, only skin distance from my wetsuit.

I could have stroked them but the strict rule was 'don't touch the mantas' because they have a protective slime covering which could be disturbed by touching them. So many people visited them every night that if human hands touched their skin they could lose this mucous layer, causing their skin to become infected. One manta kept gliding up and touching me with the tip of its wing, seemingly wanting to play as it barrelled up to brush me four or five times.

These majestic creatures are gigantic in size. Some weigh as much as a car and can grow up to 28 feet across.

Ten mantas came up to feed. It was very hard not to touch them as they all seemed to want to get up close and personal wanting to be stroked. Mantas have the largest brain of all fish. These gentle giants of the sea were really friendly and harmless. They had no teeth to speak of and luckily their tail spikes weren't venomous and their barbs had no sting.

Night Dive With the Giant Manta Rays—Hawaii ~ 2013 ~

Arching to stay back as they came up underneath me with their wide mouths open, I looked down into their cavernous throats as they swam upwards towards me. Each had a series of flapping internal gills with intricate mesh to sieve the zooplankton from the water as they swam, and they only had little teeth in their lower jaw.

In this area there were 57 'named' manta rays who visited here to feed. Each had different markings and all had been photographed and documented to be regularly monitored. On the previous night, divers saw seventeen mantas, all at once. I was thrilled with ten! I couldn't believe these enormous creatures lived on plankton alone!

Giant Manta Ray – Hawaii

I was feeling disappointed for Cam and Em sitting on the sea floor below, thinking all they could see was a distant light with specks swimming in front of it. However, their experience was equally as

The World is Your Pearl

wonderful as mine. They sat in a circle on the bottom of the sea floor with the other divers. Each of them were weighted down with a rock and held a strong spotlight. This drew the mantas to swim and trawl around them like moths to a flame.

It was a big event for all of us, and would definitely go down as one our biggest life experiences. It was a privilege to meet these gentle giants out there in the beautiful waters of the North Pacific Ocean.

CHAPTER 10

Rapture of the Shallows: Scuba Diving The South Pacific ~ 2015 ~

**Weightless
Floating in silence
Unbounded by land
The sea beckons me
~ Zen Haiku ~**

On a beautiful day in mid-March 2015, having booked and paid my deposit to join the Warby Ghostriders on yet another adventure ride, I decided I'd better get back on the bike and start training. This one was to be a 2000 kilometre ride from Amsterdam to Budapest, commencing in August.

I met with my good friend and coach, Peter Warren, at the top of Mount Evelyn to ride the 66 kilometre Warburton Trail. Though I hadn't ridden in ages I found my bike legs in no time and while speeding downhill, I saw a small scene in the distance where two dogs barked from behind a fence at a man and his little daughter who were walking their dog on the trail.

I'd turned to talk to Peter and didn't see the dog leap from its owner's grip on the leash to run over to the dogs at the fence. Mayhem unfolded when the walker's dog had been called back. The dog hadn't seen me flying downhill and I hadn't seen it returning from the side. The dog ran into my front wheel. I suddenly became airborne and hit the ground hard in an agonising crunch into the gravelly dirt, shoulder first, and skidding to take a deep layer of flesh from my leg and thigh. At the same time I sustained injuries to the same elbow which had copped five such blows on previous spills over the thousands of kilometres I'd ultimately covered. My head was saved by the helmet, which hit the ground hard, but didn't save me from the whiplash which blackened my neck with bruises.

This accident resulted in severe bruising and extreme deep-tissue damage to the right shoulder, causing two years of limited arm and shoulder use and a couple of thousand dollars in treatments.

The following day was Friday, March 13. Dosed up for pain, I went for X-rays and ultrasounds which, luckily, showed no fractures or severed tendons. Back home again, in my very dinged-up state, I made preparations for a group of 10 ladies who were to arrive that afternoon for a wedding shower I was hosting.

This was the same day when Cyclone Pam decided to hit Vanuatu in the South Pacific Ocean, packing winds of up to 320 kilometres an hour. It was a devastating monster storm which killed dozens and destroyed or damaged ninety percent of buildings in the capital.

The timing of the cyclone and the bike accident occurred two weeks before I was to depart on a scuba diving expedition. I was

Rapture of the Shallows: Scuba Diving The South Pacific ~ 2015 ~

booked on a cruise ship with the intention of diving seven islands in the South Pacific.

Now there was the chance that diving might not be an option for two reasons. Firstly, the shoulder damage might not allow me to wear the scuba gear, and secondly, of the places still available to host travellers, there might not be much left of the reefs to be seen after the cyclone.

However, it was not long later that I flew to Sydney and found myself standing on the deck of the cruise ship which stood in the dock between the Opera House and the Sydney Harbour Bridge.

With a glass of champagne in my hand, the ship departed from what would have to be one of the most spectacular harbours in the world. The ship must also have been a spectacular sight from the vantage point of the people who happened to be walking over the top of the Harbour Bridge at the same time.

I had intended to *wing it* by booking my dives once I got to each island. This advice had come from the driver who took me from the airport to the ship. He said, "That way they would be a quarter of the price." But I decided that, for travel insurance reasons, I should go through the PADDY certified dive companies used by the shipping company. This all backfired once I'd boarded the ship, when I found I could only get 'one' dive on 'one' island for the whole trip.

I immediately booked it, and paid to dive the SS President Coolidge off Santo Island, Vanuatu. However, almost immediately I received a note under my door to say the dive had been cancelled! WHAT??? I had planned this whole trip to be a diving expedition. Now suddenly there were none available!

I went down and placed a note on the public notice board asking if anyone on the ship could assist with dives and if so, to meet

The World is Your Pearl

me at 10:00 a.m. the next morning at the Anchor Bar next to the main desk.

I arrived promptly the following morning to find no one there, but overheard a man going through his hoops to one of the staff, saying, "My wife is a master diver and we've travelled from England and spent 50,000 pounds to get here so she can dive the SS President Coolidge." I had visions of Yosemite Sam wielding his guns at Bugs Bunny, ranting, "Ah paid ter see the hah divin' act, and ah plans ter see the hah divin' act"!

Deciding to get in on this act, I made myself known to them and said that I too had missed out.

He invited me to go up and meet his wife, Rita, who had her own internet coverage and was at that moment online searching for dives and I was welcome to join her. She obtained wreck dives for us on the islands of Espiritu Santo and the tiny Amadee Island off Noumea. She also secured a dive from Lifou Island, but I was unlucky as there was only one space left.

When trying to book through the ship, I'd been told the dives had been cancelled due to dangerous conditions; however, Rita found out that the dives were going ahead but had been overbooked.
Note to divers, always book ahead of your trip through a certified dive company.

Rita's dive credentials were impressive with her book of dive cards showing she was licensed for Reserve Dives, Nitrox Dives, Wreck Dives, Deep Dives, Rescue Dives, Dry Suit Dives, Peak Performance to minus 4 degrees buoyancy, Navigational Dives, Emergency First Response Dives and was a Master Diver. She had completed 256 dives. Wow! She was amazing. I only had one dive book logging twelve dives in total so far. But to clarify, I'd only just attained my International Level Two Dive Licence at the age of sixty.

Rapture of the Shallows: Scuba Diving The South Pacific ~ 2015 ~

The following morning I hopped on the tender boat to visit the Isle of Pines for some snorkelling. It was pretty under the water but there was not a lot to see in the way of sea life. As I returned, there was a group of divers in wetsuits, carrying scuba gear. I chatted to them asking what they'd seen out there. They brought out their cameras and showed me the photos and videos they'd taken of white pointer sharks and tiger sharks swimming a few feet in front of them. Such majestic creatures, I would love to have seen them.

Our conversation led to all of us linking up. I contacted Rita and we met them in a bar that night to talk dives. I was so excited to meet this group who were professionals from Sydney; each of them had made around 3000 dives all over the world. I thought it would be a dream having had so many underwater experiences.

I adore the quiet, spectacular drama of the ocean. It was so hectic getting out there and into all the heavy gear, but from the moment of submersion, the feeling of instant calm and sense of floating inside a beautiful watery world with all its strange inhabitants was like flicking a switch to euphoria, better than any drug experience I imagined there could be.

I was all set to do at least four dives, when my injured arm locked up. Frozen into the shape of a dog's hind leg. I couldn't straighten it. I must have had some floating bone fragments jamming up the joint.

I booked in to see the ship's acupuncturist. Having come all this way to dive, the outlay of $400 was worth the cost of a couple of acupuncture sessions, because they worked. I was able to straighten my arm enough to get the wetsuit and scuba gear on.

A couple of days later, Rita and I were sitting on board a tender boat heading to shore. We'd left the cruise ship to enter the Island of Luganville, in Espiritu Santo, and were taken by truck to a jetty

The World is Your Pearl

where a small boat took us out to Million Dollar Point, where the SS President Coolidge lay just off the coastline.

In World War II, a harbour and large US military base had been set up here, heavily protected by mines. Once a luxury ocean liner, the SS President Coolidge was converted into a troop ship to aid the war effort. The Coolidge's sailing orders were bungled when information about safe entry into the harbour had been accidentally omitted on her approach to Santo on October 26, 1942.

Coolidge, fearing Japanese submarines and unaware of the minefields, tried to enter the harbour, but was scuttled by their own mines. There were only two fatalities as 5400 men got safely to shore. The two men who died were a fireman, who was near the engine room and died from the first mine blast, and the captain, who had gone back to save men in the infirmary. Sadly for the captain, the men who'd been in the infirmary had already been taken to safety. He was unable to escape himself and went down with the ship.

After the war, the Americans offered all their jeeps, army tanks, trucks, bulldozers, graders, forklifts, cranes, tools and equipment to the French, asking what they would give as reasonable payment to allow them to keep it for their use on the island. Insulted by the pittance offered by the French, the Americans gave the order to drop it all into the ocean!

Now, sea creatures, corals and vegetation had established themselves inside and amongst all this equipment, as far as the eye could see.

No wonder Rita was so determined to see the remains of the SS President Coolidge. For me, it was my favourite dive so far.

This wreck was remarkable with its highest point at a depth of 66 feet, down to its deepest point at 230 feet. And it was big, VERY big. The ship was a vast expanse, almost 656 feet long, and 81 feet wide. We dropped down across the vertical deck past winches and a three-inch artillery gun with shell cases still intact beside it. Inside the hold were the remains of the washroom with taps and sinks. Under us were a jumble of jeeps, an Abraham tank, and a five-metre cannon. Inside another hold was a barber's chair. There was so much paraphernalia still sitting right where it had settled, in 1942.

Cutlery and crockery, an M-16 machine gun, gas masks and the famous White Lady statue were some of the things sitting amongst coral gardens and teeming with sea life. Among the myriad of fish I saw was a huge black-and-white lionfish and lots of beautiful little clownfish.

Between dives we ate lunch on the beach and mooched around along the shoreline, where I started collecting molten sea glass, washed up onto the shore from the burned wreck 75 years ago. Bits of old coke and beer bottles, brown medicine bottles and various bits of green, aqua and blue glass filled the front of my t-shirt.

A stranger walking on the beach asked me what I was gathering as I bulged at the front. When I showed her she kindly offered me a nylon shopping bag. I almost filled it before going back to take the second dive in another part of the vast wreck. A diver could visit twenty times and still not see everything.

Trying to bring the sea glass back on board the ship was another matter.

When it went through the security scanner I was told I couldn't bring it on board. I told the officers it was for an art installation. Amidst tittering discussions behind hands over mouths and important looks, agreeing on the fact that it was for an 'art installation' they waved it through.

The World is Your Pearl

Two days later we arrived on the Island of Lifou, in the archipelago known as the Loyalty Islands, and the spot where Rita was lucky enough to secure the last dive spot. As I watched her leave with the other divers, I took my snorkelling gear and underwater camera, and walked to the other side of the island to drop down onto a shallow reef.

Next to diving, this was one of the most enchanting things any human could do when the water was clear and the sea life was abundant. I became enraptured by everything I saw under the surface. The further I went, the bigger the drop-offs. I was mesmerised by the dazzling colours of the coral, anemones, seaweed, and sheer volume of fish shoals in all colours and sizes.

Sea turtles swam past, and I followed after them to take their photos. I kept checking my bearings, but like the paparazzi, chasing the ultimate fish photo became an obsession. I swam faster and harder to keep up with parrot and angelfish to get that perfect shot. The further I went, the bigger the fish in deeper and deeper water and the shelf life was an undisturbed splendour of sea gardens and swaying kelp, teeming with shrimp, eels and glittering, neon walls of little fishes like fists full of sequins.

In this mesmerised state, I must have lost track of time, because the next time I looked up, the island was a distant mark on the horizon. For some stupid reason, I called out in a panic. But of course I was too far out to sea for anyone but the fish to hear me. Determined not to panic, I dropped the camera to swing from its cord around my neck and hummed Dory's mantra from *Finding Nemo*. "Just keep swimming. Just keep swimming."

I was unable to swim overarm due to the severe shoulder injury. However, breast stroke was possible. Even so, I didn't seem to be moving. I realised I must have been in a current which would explain how I'd ended up so far out. Therefore, changing my direction, I swam for an indeterminate amount of time. With the firm decision I was going to survive, and utter focus, I was able to make good progress.

I had no idea how long it took, and began to wonder if the ship might already have sailed. Once back in water around 12 feet deep, it seemed barren and stewed up compared to what I'd seen out there. I found my way to shore and crossed the island to where the final people were boarding the last tender boat back to the ship. I will never know how close I came to being swept out to sea.

With everything having ended well, this experience had been great on two counts. Firstly, it was an inkling of what I'd seen in Bougainville and spent my life chasing ever since. And secondly, the scuba divers came back 'raving' about their dive. Of the 3000 dives they'd done all over the world, this had been *the* most magnificent! The abundant sea life, colours and clarity of the water for all of us in this location had been crystal clear as far as the eye could see. I was glad I hadn't simply stayed on the ship and missed this unbelievably spectacular experience.

As a result of Cyclone Pam, two of the islands we were to visit had been severely hit and were taken off the program. These were Vila Vanuatu and Mystery Island. Bloody cyclones!

We transferred to Noumea and travelled by bus to where we took a RIB (Rigid Inflatable Boat) to the exquisite Amedee Island. The aqua sea lapped the fine sand of its shores, and shady trails led through lush tropical vegetation to a beautiful white lighthouse. We walked along a boardwalk to the Amedee Diving Club hut to fill out paperwork and grab scuba gear, then out along the jetty again to the RIB, which took us to the ToHo 5 dive spot.

The World is Your Pearl

On the sea floor at a depth of around 72 feet was a pretty little fishing wreck. We dived around inside the hull and up to the crow's nest. There were lots of big fish, three white-tipped reef sharks, eagle rays, lionfish, trigger fish, lizard fish, groupers and big eels. Although the water was slightly murky it was great to see so many fish varieties. Back on the island for lunch we played with a female sea snake who lived under the slatted floor of the dive hut, where suspended day beds, cloth chairs and hammocks swung in the tropical breeze.

There was no accommodation here. People came by boat on day trips to go swimming and snorkelling with the sea turtles. The dive after lunch was on the Passepe Boulari reef. Down again into the beautiful world under the sea I swam amongst the reef sharks, spotted rays, Napoleon wrasse and blue-spotted coronet fish.

It took such a lot to get out to these places via an array of planes, ships, trucks, vans and little boats. However, these moments of

Rapture of the Shallows: Scuba Diving The South Pacific ~ 2015 ~

ecstasy, seeing such creatures in their watery environments, could never be forgotten.

This trip for me was a meditation. When at home, my life was filled with 'things' and 'busy-ness'! Here I knew no-one. My room back on the ship was silent except for the beautiful hissing sound of the sea. I was out of contact, with no phone or internet; not even my phone data worked for games or texts.

There was a real swell where we were positioned out on the Pacific Ocean today. The coat hangers were rocking in the wardrobe and it was too windy to sit on the balcony. However, with my room position being mid-ship and the wonderful ship's stabilisers, I didn't have any feeling of turbulence or sea sickness. There were plenty of shipboard activities available, but it was rare not to have any pressing calendar events, and I was happy to sit in silence with my own company for a while.

The south-east trade winds blew steadily year-round under the influence of cyclones and tropical lows. Vanuatu was the most hurricane-prone country in the South Pacific. I learned that between 1970 and 1985, no fewer than 29 hurricanes struck Vanuatu on average, and that any given location can be hit by a hurricane every other year, usually between January and April. These had been becoming stronger and more frequent in recent years.

A year after this dive trip, my collection of sea glass was put to good use. Interspersed with other bits of brightly coloured pieces left over from previous glass projects, all were incorporated on the outside of a large, round fishbowl to create a dazzling table lamp.

Now the spectacular sea rubble from this majestic shipwreck is an individual art piece.

The World is Your Pearl

Rapture of the Shallows: Scuba Diving The South Pacific ~ 2015 ~

Sea glass lamp

I want to age like sea glass.
Smoothed by tides,
but not broken.
I want my hard edges to soften.
I want to ride the waves
and go with the flow.
I want to catch a wave
and let it carry me
to where I belong.
I want to be picked up
and held gently by
those who delight in my
well-earned patina and
appreciate the changes I went
through to achieve that beauty.
I want to enjoy the journey
and always remember that if
you give the ocean something
breakable it will turn it into
something beautiful.
I want to age like sea glass.

~ Bernadette Noll ~

CHAPTER 11

Rapid Adventure Ladakh ~ July 2015 ~

*Today is the greatest day I've ever known..
Can't live for tomorrow; tomorrow's much too long.
'Smashing Pumpkins'
~ Toilet door, Italy ~*

t was an accident.

Having collected the mail from my letterbox, there was a large book from World Expeditions advertising upcoming adventures. I didn't plan to look at it as I had recently cancelled the 2000 kilometre ride from Amsterdam to Budapest due to the bike accident, and I was still badly injured.

However, I *accidentally* tore it open, and there was Mary Moody, offering to guide travellers on a yoga trek through the Indian Himalayas, commencing in Delhi and travelling across to Leh for a trek through Ladakh, ending with a flight to Srinagar to unwind and luxuriate in Kashmir on ornate and palatial 70-year-old house boats.

At that moment I decided, what the heck? One more challenging adventure wouldn't hurt. After all, I *could* walk. There would be plenty of time for sedate activity when I was dead!

The world's weather had been crazy. Just prior to my last adventure, diving in the South Pacific Ocean in March 2015, Cyclone Pam had wiped out Vila Vanuatu and Mystery Island, among many others, which necessitated a change of itinerary. Then in April 2015, devastating earthquakes destroyed vast areas of Nepal, killing 10,000 people and injuring 23,000.

A further earthquake in the Indian Himalayas was followed by a heatwave in Delhi in May 2015, which killed 2500 people throughout Northern India.

This was five weeks before I would be leaving the cold of Melbourne's winter in July to fly to Delhi where the temperature would still be 40 to 45 degrees, then continue up to Leh the next day to an altitude of 11,483 feet, in temperatures sometimes below zero for seventeen days. There would be cold nights and *hopefully* sunny days, then back down to Delhi for five days, where the temperature may be around 40 degrees by then, and home to mid-winter in Melbourne by August.

Just getting over there was a feat of endurance in itself and typical of most travel. As the flight from Melbourne to Delhi was to depart at 7:00 a.m., I needed to leave home by 3:00 a.m., so travelled to stay by the airport overnight for ease of an early departure. The flight was delayed until 9:30 a.m. but didn't actually depart until 10:30 a.m. On arrival at Delhi we circled for 40 minutes due to monsoon rains and got into the hotel at 10:00 p.m. India time.

Rapid Adventure Ladakh ~ July 2015 ~

Tired and dizzy with exhaustion, I was warmly greeted by Mary and our yoga instructor, Jan. It was a relief to get into bed for two hours before a wakeup call at 1:45 a.m. I had to leave by 2:30 a.m. for a 5:50 a.m. flight to Leh which left at 6:45 a.m.

Because I'd joined this trip at the last minute, the other members of the group were booked on another airline. I was to fly alone to meet them in Leh.

Once transferred to Delhi airport, it was mayhem. No wonder I had to be there so early. I queued in mile-long queues for ages. There were no overhead signs which worked, except for one which said, 'India Airport is a clean airport'. Another said, 'This is a silent area'. There were no flight announcements. No-one knew anything. I was eventually matched up with others flying to Leh, and we stood for a further one and a half hours while one person processed the entire flight.

After massive security checks with boots off and being frisked in the 'women's area' I went to the allocated gate on my boarding pass. It was no surprise to learn that the flight was delayed yet again. While queuing to board the plane, the attendant said, "Run! Your gate was changed." My throat and chest were burning as I jogged for fifteen minutes to Gate 65. I was on my own and panicking.

As I ran, I came up to two pilots and asked them how much further it was to Gate 65. They said, "You can rest now, we'll take you." They were my pilots. They took my bag. Boarding had long closed, but they ushered me through. One of them asked if I was alone. I said I was part of a group of 16 flying on another airline. He asked which airline. I didn't know. He said, "Because we are the only aircraft going. All the others have been cancelled due to the extreme weather. No other pilot will go to 10,000 feet in these conditions."

The World is Your Pearl

Oh great!

It was a one-hour-45-minute flight. The air was thin and turbulent at altitude at the best of times. The pilot went on to say, "There's a 50/50 chance we won't make it."

That was unnerving.

He laughed and said, "There's a big chance we won't be able to land and we'll have to turn around and go back."

During the flight we were told it would be six degrees at our destination.

After a smooth landing through one of the narrowest mountain passes in the world, I was enraptured. One minute I was looking down on glaciers and the vast snow-capped mountains of the great Himalayan Range, the next there was a wall of rock on either side of the aircraft.

The Leh airport was a tiny shed surrounded by shale rock mountains with distant stupas, monasteries and palaces. The people here were different. They all seemed very open, relaxed, and warm-hearted. Many were either trekkers or Sherpas.

Leh is the capital of Ladakh, a country renowned for its remote mountain beauty and culture, and sometimes called 'Little Tibet' as it had been strongly influenced by Tibetan culture. Once a Buddhist kingdom, it was the highest plateau of the Indian state of Kashmir, bordering Tibet to the east.

Having been transported to the hotel, I was immediately greeted by a huge Sikh, who put his arms around me and gave me a hug. His name was Raj and he was to be our guide for the duration of the trek.

Rapid Adventure Ladakh ~ July 2015 ~

Mary and the others were already there. (The pilot must have thought he was a real jokester.) The group had flown in before me and had watched my plane circling.

Mary was so pleased to see me. She was happy once all her chickens were under her wing. We ate breakfast at 8:30 a.m. and had cups of tea, then I was shown to a large, ground-floor room, which looked out to the snow-capped peaks of the Himalayan glaciers beyond a rose garden. At last I could settle in to rest. This hotel would be home for a couple of days while we acclimatised to the altitude.

At lunch I discovered our group number had reduced by two, as one person had sustained a last-minute injury and the other had been deemed medically unfit for the degree of difficulty we were facing. There would now be 13 trekkers. Along with me were Julie, Niall, Ruth, Rose, Diane, Marie, Sue, Jan, John, his son Campbell, two Belindas, Mary, Jan the yoga instructor, our leader Raj, and Lobzang our guide, bringing the total to 17, excluding the many Sherpas, cooks and pack horses.

Lobzang was a young local man studying commerce at university. As for Nepal, to try to get ahead, the young men had to earn money as Sherpas or guides for many months of the year.

After lunch I had a rest before joining the group for yoga on a grassy area high above a roaring river. I discovered that, as well as for cycling, my yoga days would be over for a very long time. The shoulder injury I sustained 16 weeks ago had stifled a lot of movement, though I did what I could.

The following day we journeyed to the Leh Palace and the ancient Victory Fort, which had been built in the 17th century to commemorate Ladakh's independence from invading armies from Baltistan and Kashmir.

The World is Your Pearl

**Leh Palace.
Photo Mike Litchfield**

I was feeling ill due to the altitude, with really bad headaches, nausea and unsteady on my feet. Everyone felt the same. Painkillers were the only option at this stage. Although I had tablets for altitude sickness, they were not recommended to be taken yet as they masked the symptoms, which could be deadly. Outside my room were facilities for decompression, an oxygen tank and mask.

Overseas trips always took a bit of winding into. The sheer drama of flights, customs, forms, endless queues and hold-ups were hard work, but I was thinking it was all going to be worth it. We were asleep by 8:30 p.m., and, after a night of pouring rain and thunderstorms, we all felt much better in the morning, even though the headaches and altitude issues still continued.

After a very early breakfast, we journeyed for around an hour to visit the imposing Thikse Temple. This was the wealthiest monastery in Ladakh, home to both male and female monks. It was magnificently adorned with colourful paintings, mandalas, wood and brass prayer wheels. The floors of the inner sanctum where the Dalai Lama sits were of ancient stone and timbers, worn smooth by bare feet over hundreds of years. Incense burned and yak butter lamps glowed with a golden light, as offerings of water and soft drinks, cookies, flowers, chocolate, lollies and money were placed on Buddha's altar.

From this high vantage point, the vast imposing landscape stretched far below through green valleys and beyond to snow-capped mountain ranges. The clouds lifted, as beautiful warm sunlight shone through a magnesium-blue sky, intensifying the colours of everything around us.

There were fish ponds in the flatlands of the valley. The fish were not eaten, but the pond water was reticulated and used as fertiliser on crops. Ladakh only receives 100 ml of water per annum, so they were pleased about the rain they'd been having as there were only four months of growing season per year to harvest straw for fodder, mud brick making, and fuel for fires when they were snowed in during winter.

The mud brick houses were very strong with flat roofs. When it snowed in winter, it insulated them against the freezing, minus 30 degree temperatures outside, acting like an igloo. In many places I was interested to see ornately carved rocks sitting in piles along the roadsides.

Travelling back, we passed the private residence of the Dalai Lama. Surprisingly, it was a very modest house with a beautiful yellow roof, and set amongst trees in a lush green valley.

This had already been a big morning, but we stopped again to climb more steep stone steps to visit the Shey Palace which originally

The World is Your Pearl

housed the Ladakh royal family. Within the palace temple was the oldest stupa, beautifully whitewashed and topped with old gold.

Inside all the temples we visited were giant Buddhas made of clay, ornately painted and also embellished with gold.

At each monastery we removed our boots to visit the sacred interiors.

As I looked out to the stunning views below, all over the valley there was a huge amount of real estate development being established everywhere. The allotment boundaries were laid out with rows of painted white stones about the size of footballs. Massive stockpiles of handmade mud bricks were stacked in preparation for building.

Enquiring about the thousands of mud bricks, I asked Raj whether people ever stole any. He didn't understand. I said, "Is there any theft here?" He still didn't get what I meant. I said, "If I left a pile of money on a fence post, would someone take it?" Oh, *now* he got it! "No, there is no stealing here, no-one steals." In this society there was no theft *'ever'!*

I adored these people. They were sweet and gentle and honest, most of them deeply embedded in the Buddhist religion. The children looked proud in their school uniforms, and felt it a privilege to go to school.

We got back quite late to a hot lunch of an array of flavoursome dishes. We ate mostly vegetarian with a small amount of chicken. Meals were a selection of up to ten or twelve freshly made dishes. As well, there were flatbreads, made on the spot, along with papadams, which we learned were to be eaten at the end of the meal to aid digestion.

Rapid Adventure Ladakh ~ July 2015 ~

The flatbreads (naan) could be filled with beans or squares of goat milk cheese cooked in a spicy tomato sauce. They were delicious with all the flavours from the sauce of so many dishes. Potato patties, lentils, green spinach, creamy and flavoursome eggplant, and a mild curried chicken dish, like butter chicken. Marsala tea was served with hot milk, followed by plates of sliced melons and various fruits. Huge amounts of leafy greens, fruits and vegetables were freshly grown in the fertile valleys.

After lunch I wandered out with a few of the others to see the local handcrafts. We looked at jewellery, hair ornaments and artefacts made from silver, copper and brass, inlaid with coral and turquoise, leather pouches, wallets and book covers.

Once again, the headaches, made worse by diesel fumes from old vehicles chugging up and down the streets, caused me to give in and return to my room.

As most of the shops and stalls were open until 10:00 p.m., I ventured out again after dinner. Labourers still worked away in the dark, mixing cement or concrete on big plastic sheets. Each sheet was held by a man at each corner as the mortar was mixed and scooped into a bowl, then handed to another man, to be tipped out and spread to make the floor of yet another little roadside shop.

There was no street lighting and the footpaths were treacherous with gaping holes, so big a person could fall into them in the dark without good night eyes. Tourism had changed Ladakh forever. The progress taking place was non-stop. At one time, the people had been self-sufficient, relying on four months a year to grow and harvest crops. If one village struck hard times, the next village came to their aid. Everyone worked together, and life hummed away in peace and harmony. Tourism through adventure travel had opened many opportunities for them in different ways.

The World is Your Pearl

Early the next morning, the sun was shining brightly when we met for our yoga session in the large courtyard. The air was fresh and fragrant, and we were surrounded by colourful garden beds which faced the snow-capped Himalayan Mountain range. Yoga breaths were inhaled under an intensely vivid blue sky.

We were all feeling much better now, and I enjoyed the yoga, even with my 'broken wing'. After breakfast we journeyed out in cars, past miles of military establishments and army trucks. Huge numbers of soldiers were in force to keep peace against Pakistan who had been at war for so long. Kashmir had only recently opened its borders for Westerners to be able to enter in the last two years.

Travelling through the Indus pass, where the mighty Indus River flowed all the way to Pakistan, we arrived in Phyang to witness the very grand monastic festival which occurred once a year. The temple itself was imposing with its stark whitewashed walls, made more blinding white against a violet blue sky.

Inside was a beautiful throne where the highest lama sat. We went to look inside other temples built in the 17th century. It was cool and dark inside these interiors, which were adorned with paintings from the same period. Down the hill, in a large square between the monastery buildings, lamas and monks performed sacred dances and dramas all day in the hot sun.

Their elaborate costumes were extraordinary, and included huge, heavy masks with faces of gods, spirits or animals. These were made of painted wood, heavy felt, or beaten metal. Many were hung with tassels, hair or fibres to represent fur. The garments were heavy, comprising enormous layers of quilted silks and satins, embellished with symbolic embroideries and appliqué.

Supporting the dancers and performers were musicians, dressed in full regalia. They played ancient horns, drums and clanging, jangling instruments in seemingly discordant notes. On the main centre podium sat the high priests in traditional robes. Their heads were adorned with magnificent, spartan-like headdresses.

**Phyang Tsedup festival
Photos – Niall MacNeill**

The World is Your Pearl

We ate boxed picnic lunches in the shade on the steps of a stupa while some of our group went in to chant and meditate with one of the lamas.

This day had been an immense experience.

We returned to our hotel and I took a walk through the streets of Leh where I saw a shopfront offering white water rafting at a cost equivalent to the tiny sum of AU$25! Included in the price were pick-up from our hotel at 9:00 a.m., transport to the start of the rapids, provision of wetsuits, helmets and booties, rafting from 11:00 a.m. till 3:00 p.m., late lunch with refreshments and transport back to our hotels. This would have cost upwards of $200 anywhere else. What a bargain!

I went back to meet the others for dinner and asked the crowd if anyone would join me the next day. Thinking I was crazy, no-one spoke, as our trek was to start early the following morning. After another minute, Campbell, the youngest of our group, said he'd be interested. He was 17 years old.

"Anyone else?" Niall volunteered. I talked his wife, Ruth, into joining us.

There had been no way of looking up reviews on this rafting company as the entire town was experiencing no internet. However, the four of us walked back to the booking office in town after dinner, took a chance and purchased our tickets. As we returned through the choking traffic we stopped to buy cheap sunglasses for the rafting, then went back to the hotel to arrange wakeup calls.

At 4:45 a.m. everyone woke in time to be taken back to the magnificent Tikse temple where we climbed its many steep steps to the top of the very high monastery roof. Two monks stood towards the edge, and blew into horns several feet long. These deep, resonant sounds were the call to prayer, far across what felt like the entire world below. It was a gloriously clear morning with the saffron and burgundy robes of the monks contrasting against the green of the sweeping valley to the crisp white of the glaciers.

All was silent except for the reverberating horn sounds, and the distant twitter of little birds which I couldn't see. It was one of the most unique experiences to ever encounter.

We climbed back down the ancient wooden steps to enter an inner prayer chamber where we assembled quietly along the back wall. The throne in this inner room was where the Dalai Lama sat when he was here. His photograph hung behind the throne. At 6:00 a.m. all the monks from the monastery filed in to the sounds of ancient musical symbols, drums and horns. Mantras were chanted as incense burned and little novice monks, small boys perhaps 8 or 10 years old, waited on their elders, serving yak butter tea with huge scoops of toasted barley powder and milk curds in lovely clay bowls.

Before early morning prayers – Tikse Temple
Photo – Niall MacNeill

The World is Your Pearl

The prayers and meditations were to last until 10:00 a.m.; however, we quietly removed ourselves to tip-toe down many more steps to the temple courtyard where, with prior permission from the high lama, we performed our yoga practice. The little monks stood staring. They'd never seen anything like this. I glimpsed one young monk taking a photo with his mobile phone from a high balcony.

Novice monks watching our yoga practice – Tikse Temple

Rapid Adventure Ladakh ~ July 2015 ~

We four River Rafters left quickly, taking the first driver to travel the long distance back. We returned by 8:30 a.m. and collected our picnic breakfasts from the dining room staff in time for our 9:00 a.m. pick-up.

The four of us were greeted at the front of the hotel by our driver who took us to our 'transport' which turned out to be a *shocker!* An ancient, rickety old bus spewing diesel fumes which had to be endured as we travelled the hour and a half journey to Chilling.

We arrived there to a spot where a sharp hairpin bend led down to the river. The driver had to do a possible 13 point turn to get around. We careened down the hill to a tattered marquee by the water's edge. River guides issued us with thin, torn and threadbare 'wet' suits, filled with so many holes they looked like survivors of shark attacks.

To complete the ensemble, we were fitted with similarly worn booties and dinged-up helmets. Back on the bus, we drove a few feet and were asked to get out and walk up the hill to the hairpin bend. The bus didn't have the power to ascend the shallow incline with the weight of 12 passengers.

Back on board, we set out for another hour of one of the hairiest rides of our lives along a narrow dirt road freshly dug out of the steep, shale rock mountainside. It was almost vertical above and below us as it dropped away to the Indus River 300 feet below.

People were working, almost entirely by hand, breaking and moving rock. Many were women, shrouded in saris, sitting in the dirt and labouring away with babies swaddled in front of them, or toddlers with little eyes red from the heat and dust.

It was pitiful to see, *when I could actually open my eyes*, as the ride was so terrifying that I could hardly look, much less take photos or video footage of the road conditions. I had a front window seat with a view of the river below, as the wheels of the bus crunched along almost non-existent edges which crumbled as we passed, sending rocks and stones cascading off towards the river below.

I couldn't imagine how a road could even exist here with the never-ending evidence of constant landslides. It was hair-raising, and I nearly had a heart attack as large rusty trucks and digging machines passed us on the inside. On the perimeters of numerous bends, little rows of stones were placed to warn that these were 'soft edges'. The trip was harrowing.

In just over an hour, we stopped on the side of the road and were directed to a small concrete toilet block where we could get into our bathing gear and wetsuits. Back on the bus we travelled a bit further to a steep roadside embankment where we clambered down about 50 feet to the edge of the river.

Several faded inflatable boats were being held in the water by our river guides who issued us with faded 'designer grunge' life vests. After a lot of hesitation by the twelve participants I volunteered to be the demo dummy, required to fall backwards off one of the boats and be safely hauled back, in rescue mode.

After a full safety briefing, we headed off. The level 3 rapids were classified as intermediate. There were moderate, irregular waves which were often difficult to avoid and which would sometimes swamp our boat. Complex manoeuvres were required in the fast currents, and good boat control was often needed, as we were issued with lots of loud instructions to "Paddle forward"; "Stop"; "Forward"; "Faster, faster"; "Left oar"; "Stop"; "Get down"; "Lock feet". On we went through spinning whirlpools, roiling over areas called 'rooster tails' and sloshing through others termed as 'washing machines'.

Rapid Adventure Ladakh ~ July 2015 ~

The water of the Indus was glacially cold and fast-moving. The churning rapids were intermittently spaced between drifts of glass-smooth, calm water with little eddies and whirlpools. For 28 kilometres, this stop-start experience was exhilarating as our guides yelled to everyone to paddle like crazy, to navigate through the churning white water, then out again to drift along stretches of calm.

The river was flanked by cavernous mountains of shale and sheer rock faces which soared in some places to a thousand feet towards the sky. In the quiet moments, we looked up to see the vehicles traversing the road we'd travelled along to get to the start point. We now had the chance to take in the gravity of how precarious we'd been as we'd driven over the 'outside' sections of this perilous stretch of road. We were peering up to the *underside* of overhangs which would have been the areas where the little rows of stones were set to warn drivers to steer clear.

The facts and figures of death rates due to trucks, buses and vehicles going over the edges here are almost non-existent, though the locals say it happens "a lot". As we came out of the rapids at the end, we drifted to the centre of a very wide stretch of river where our rescue kayakers fooled around and flipped themselves in their boats over and over and came up again. With the addition of other kayak groups on the river, the rafters totalled 30. Our river guide, Sambo, yelled, "Thirty in a row; one roll for everyone who jumps in."

Although the river was the colour of milky mud, many jumped out of their boats to frolic in the icy water before we were taken to the opposite embankment to leave our boats at the spot where we'd been issued with our leaky wetsuits that morning, and to the end of our rafting experience. It had been marvellous.

We'd had a ball. All the muddy, sandy wetsuits were dumped in a bin for someone to clean, then, dressed again, we were taken to an old marquee and treated to a surprisingly sumptuous lunch of

The World is Your Pearl

vegetarian dishes, fresh salads and milky Marsala tea. Back on the rickety bus, we were once again asked to alight and walk up the stiff hill while the driver chugged past us and did his 13 point turn. We hopped back on the bus amidst its cloud of diesel fumes, to return to Leh.

As we passed the never-ending military bases, queues of civilians stretched for huge distances along the compound roadsides. They had been there when we passed in the morning. The queues were still there at 5:30 p.m. I found out they were there for employment.

The army controls the road building and maintenance of areas washed away by landslides and waterfalls. Other job opportunities included a multitude of tasks such as cooking and cleaning for the soldiers.

As we'd lived to tell the tale, we all agreed this experience had certainly been value for money. This had been the perfect start to our adventure.

CHAPTER 12

Trekking Ladakh— An Epic Journey ~ 2015 ~

*Don't pray for an easy life,
pray for the strength to endure a hard one.
~ Bruce Lee ~*

Our trek began, following an early morning transfer in a convoy of four 4WDs. As our vehicles snaked around the narrow roads, we looked down on the River Indus below while climbing up through a steep pass to Zinchen, a small settlement to the south of the Indus Valley where our crew were assembled with ponies and pack horses to carry our gear for the next few days.

The Indus civilisation was the oldest in the world. They stopped being nomadic 2000 years ago when they discovered the benefits of communal living, working together to grow crops and keep livestock. Ladakh sat in the Trans-Himalaya region, a rugged land of high passes that crossed the great Himalaya and the Zanskar

The World is Your Pearl

The pack horses

Range. In the depths of the valleys, tiny settlements thrived in oases within an otherwise arid landscape, known as the cold desert or alpine desert.

Road signs along the winding roads were amusing: 'Blow horn on my curves'; 'Better Mister Late than Mister Never'; 'Drive with care—Accident rare'; 'Three enemies of the road—Drink, Speed and Overload'; "Life is short. Don't make it shorter'; 'Speed Thrills but Kills'; 'After whiskey, driving risky'.

Although the vehicles had actually brought us down a bit to 12,000 feet, I was still finding it hard to breathe. It was searing hot and the going was hard after my exertion on the river yesterday. We headed out on foot up a spectacular gorge towards our campsite which was below the village of Rumbak at 12,699 feet. We had a wonderful view towards the Stok Kangri Glacier at 19,685 feet.

Trekking Ladakh—An Epic Journey ~ 2015 ~

The heat became worse and we stopped at a small treed oasis to eat our lunch and take a siesta before heading up again to ascend a further 8202 feet, only two and half kilometres, before stopping again where we took off our shirts to wet them in the river. This made the walk to camp a little easier.

We came upon a herd of blue sheep. They were wild sheep, native to this area, and famous for their blue horns. In the colder seasons ibex also lived here along with snow leopards which had only recently been rediscovered after being deemed extinct. We were in a cold desert, and were shown a bush which the snow leopards ate if they couldn't find prey, as they were omnivorous.

Up here at altitude, there were red wolves, foxes, marmots, goats, deer, yaks and vultures.

Each morning we were woken in our tents with a cup of tea and a bowl of warm water for washing. In the morning our early morning yoga was spectacular. With the vast rocky mountains soaring around us, we spread our mats on lush green grass and moved through our practice with the sun on our backs to the hollow munching sounds of the tethered donkeys, yaks and pack horses as they grazed among us, tinkling the bells around their necks. The only other sound was the occasional drone of a heavy bumble bee as it foraged in the wildflowers.

The day's trek was only three hours to the next camp where we would stay for two nights while we acclimatised. Once again, the crew went ahead and had our tents up by the time we'd arrived. From here we undertook day walks to Rumbak village and the side valley leading to the base of the Tok La which afforded spectacular views of the Trans-Himalaya.

The altitude was having all sorts of effects on everyone. Our lung capacities took a long time to adjust to the thin air. As we climbed, our lungs coped less and less the thinner the air became. I wasn't sure if I had flu symptoms. My nostrils were dry to the point of bleeding due to the dry air and dust. I had a sore throat and a lack of energy, making walking a struggle, which was unusual for me. My headaches had reduced a bit, though I felt fuzzy and light-headed. However, I plodded slowly and enjoyed a lovely walk through the valley. Fortunately the heat wasn't severe.

Ladakh was situated deep in the Himalayas on the western edge of the Tibetan plateau. It was one of the highest and driest inhabited regions on earth. Scorched by the sun in summer, frozen solid for eight months of winter, it seemed to be a place which couldn't sustain human life. Yet over the centuries, fields had been carved out of the rocks and sand of the desert, which enabled the people not only to survive but to prosper.

With only 10 cm of rainfall a year, the people of Ladakh had to rely instead on glacial melt water which was brought to the fields through an elaborate system of channels, often many kilometres long. The villages were at altitude between 11,483 feet and 13,123 feet, where the growing season was extremely short. At slightly lower elevations, orchards of apple and apricot trees grew.

The people of Ladakh were lovely. When they harvested their crops in the valley farms, they preferred to work together on one person's field then move onto that of the next family, singing as they worked. Their beasts of labour were sung to as they pulled ploughs. It was so pleasant to see and hear. Much nicer than the welding of a whip or putting fear into them. The people of Ladakh were more like Tibetans in temperament. I saw the difference immediately on the day I flew in from Delhi to Leh. As soon as I landed in Leh, all faces were peaceful, gentle and smiling with a certain inner calm.

It seemed to me like a nirvana, where, with few exceptions, basic needs were met within the community. This was a timeless life where work and leisure were one. Making the most of the resources around them, almost everything that grew wild was gathered and put to use for fodder or medicine, fence making or basket weaving. Everyday life in the village was based on a close relationship between people and the earth. This living experience of interconnectedness was reinforced by the teaching of Buddhism. The religion permeated all aspects of life. Almost every village had its own monastery and the landscape was dotted with stupas.

Every community had three stupas. Dome-shaped buildings erected as Buddhist shrines painted in yellow, white and blue. These colours represented the three elements. The tops were yellow or gold, representing wisdom and ethical conduct. Middle sections were white, for compassion and mental purification, and the bases were blue for strength and power.

These monuments represented the essence of Buddhist philosophy. This interdependence was the basis of everything in the universe. At the top of the stupa, a crescent moon cradled the sun, symbolising the oneness of all life. Even the sun and the moon which seemed so far apart were inextricably related. Interdependence was very important in all things. Everyone and everything came into being through dependence and relations. The animals relied on the plants. The plants depended on the soil. Humans depended on the basic elements of air, water, animals and plants. All things were interrelated and interconnected.

The small scale of the economy helped to strengthen community ties. People had the security of knowing they could depend on one another. The animals of an entire village were attended by just a few villagers at a time, who shared the work on a rotational basis. Everyone took turns. At all births, marriages and deaths, everyone provided feasts and performed rituals together which gave them a sense of belonging to something larger than themselves. If there was trouble, they made sure it was settled in order to reach a

The World is Your Pearl

compromise before it got any worse. The biggest insult you could give anyone was to say they had a bad temper.

Nestled into the landscape, houses were built from wood and handmade mud bricks. They sat within rock-walled compounds amidst beautiful fields of corn, barley, wheat and vegetable crops. Agricultural work was founded on cooperation. Labour, animal power and farm implements were routinely shared. In that way the farming was done on a very cooperative basis. All the families helped each other. That way no money was spent. There were no cash payments, only food was served. Everyone helped for free. Neighbours and relatives came, even from far away.

For eight months of the year, throughout the harsh winter, people and animals were shut inside their houses. The animals created warmth from the ground storey below. In the spring and summer the families sowed their seed, harvested vegetables and fruit to store, gathered wood and cow-dung to dry in the sun to use as cooking fuel, and fodder was cut to store up for the animals.

The Ladakh lady was the head of the family. The senior matriarch had complete superiority over all males. Girls were a last resource in the family line. In order to keep power in one hand and to control the distribution of land, the boys always inherited, and the girls received a dowry.

In the remote areas of Ladakh, polygamy was the practice to keep the population down; a woman had two or three husbands.

As we arrived at camp, the weather had turned. The wind blew up to the point of almost blowing the tents away. We ran for cover as the mess tent kept losing pegs in the violent wind. It poured rain throughout the night and I couldn't sleep as I struggled for breath and had another thumping headache.

Trekking Ladakh—An Epic Journey ~ 2015 ~

The next morning I got up and took a painkiller as I heaved for air trying to do the yoga. At breakfast time I was still in my tent, scrabbling around trying to pack while everyone had almost finished eating their breakfast in the mess tent. Julie, one of our trekking group, noticed my unusual inaction and offered to help me pack up my gear. She stuffed my sleeping bag for me while Campbell did up my bag. Campbell was an amazing person. He was trekking with his dad, John. Campbell was very quiet but constantly pitched in to help the Sherpas, pull down and put up tents, or help people across rivers. I was in awe of his helpfulness as a young person. He was a very decent human being.

It was definitely time for me to start the altitude tablets. I took one and *just* had time to grab the dregs of porridge and some vegemite toast before we headed out at 9:00 a.m. Today was to be another short day. We followed a trail which wound up past a solitary stone house at Yurutse to our camp at 14,272 feet at the base of the approach to the Ganda La. This was a much more challenging climb which headed way above the scree slopes where we had views back down the Indus Valley and across the high peaks which formed the Stok Kangri Range. We walked up the valley and climbed a further 500 feet. I was glad my altitude tablet kicked in. It eventually afforded me enough breath for the climb.

The ledges and paths were very narrow and steep in places and we had to scramble up the slope to get out of the way of our pack horses as they clanked past with their big bells.

Crossing several fast-flowing streams, we were aided by the men of our group who moved rocks, and juggled debris for us to step on to assist us over. We arrived into camp early, as the Sherpas were putting up our tents.

The mess tent had been the first to go up and the cooks had a hot lunch ready for us to sit down to as soon as we came in.

The World is Your Pearl

It amazed me that, although we were often on almost vertical slopes, our crew found places to pitch our tents which were on almost flat sections of the mountainside. It was probably the case that we were so tired at the end of a day's trekking that we could possibly have slept standing up. However, I don't recall having spent an uncomfortable night where I felt I was slipping downhill.

As I washed my clothes in the river, the skies over the snow-capped glaciers turned black. Everyone battened down the hatches and we all hunkered down in our tents while Lobzang hurriedly hacked away to dig trenches around them. He and Campbell and some of the crew worked like crazy as the rain suddenly started to pour.

It became freezing. I couldn't get warm, so I put on everything, including layers of merino, thermal and polar fleece tops, track pants, possum fur socks and gloves, beanie and neck warmer, and got into my sleeping bag. The storm was violent with lightning, torrential rain, and massive thunder which shook the earth. It must have continued for two hours as I fell into a deep sleep. Mary woke me by yelling, "Are you okay, Glenda?"

I opened the zip to my tent and blinked out at her from my toasty warm cocoon like a bear coming out of hibernation, to view a sea of mud. The river further up the valley had broken and redirected its flow right in the direction of our camp. We were lucky not to have been flushed off down the mountain.

Some other trekkers further down the mountain were not so lucky. As the storm hit, they had been forced to trudge up through the pass in the pouring rain while our group were snug and dry in our tents.

We had been amazingly lucky with the timing of bad weather, though the next day was supposed to be really hard and it would be extremely slippery and muddy. I'd picked a bad time to get an upset stomach. Everything was going through me. I was told it was a result of the altitude and possibly the change of food on my system.

Everybody sang in Ladakh. I was woken at 5:00 a.m. by the chant-singing of the Sherpas cooking our breakfast. They often preferred to sleep outside on the ground. It must have been close to zero throughout the night. They slept on the dirt floor of the mess tent. By 5:30 a.m., our cups of tea and wash bowls were brought to our tents amidst a sea of mud, like coffee cream. By now it had stopped raining and the cloud was lifting.

As our tents were being pulled down and packed onto the horses, we set out and climbed up along the donkey trails, for a further 500 feet to where yaks and cross-bred domesticated dzos were grazing. Dzos were a cross between a cow and a yak. They were very docile and hard-working.

With a sudden new-found energy, and without realising it, I was well ahead of the group. I climbed way up to where a pale yak sat with its coat seeming to glisten like gold in the sun, his face like a gentle Buddha. Suddenly Mary was screaming out and gesticulating from below: "Glenda, come back." I took some photos of him then turned and ran down the hill to the others. Mary was beside herself, saying, "Look at all the calves everywhere. They're being protected by the male bull. There are a million ##*# photos of yaks on ##*# Google!" I was in trouble. Mary was *very* upset.

I think the story I'd told the group a few days before regarding the horrendous experience of the lady who'd attempted to pat a wild yak in Nepal had totally freaked Mary out. She must have had visions of a similar thing happening. However, I was nowhere even close to this yak, who was lying down with his legs tucked under him. He got up in time for me to take a standing shot before I high-tailed it down the mountain, back to the group.

The World is Your Pearl

Five years later, Mary wrote of this episode of the trek in her book *The Accidental Tour Guide*, where she said in retrospect, amidst all the drama, she hadn't even thought to take photos herself of the yak herd and would probably have to ask *me* for one! This prompted me to look back over the archives to find the famous yak photos, which amazed me. While on the side of that mountain, I must have been looking through rose-coloured glasses or dazzled by the sun that day, because the 'lovely' yak I remembered was just a dirty old moth-eaten thing which only a mother could love, and certainly not worthy of Mary's near heart attack.

The famous YAK

Trekking Ladakh—An Epic Journey ~ 2015 ~

We continued our gradual ascent to the Ganda La, higher and higher for a further 600 feet to eventually reach a height of 16,207 feet, with breathtaking views of the Stok Range. A couple of us seemed to fly up ahead of the others. Niall and I arrived first, and stood in the gap at the top of the pass which was the highest point of the trail. There was a stupa there, with its prayer flags fluttering in the wind. Niall and I decided to scramble up the final 50 metres to reach the 16,404 feet mark. (This was 5000 metres.)

I climbed almost to the top then 'froze' as I'd taken the wrong direction by a few feet and ran out of places to hang on to. I hung there for ten minutes while Niall went to the top and took photographs. As he descended, he came around behind and released me from my stricken terror. These situations happen whenever my brain goes into lockdown with vertigo. It only takes a touch to snap me out of it. Back down at the stupa, the others were arriving and high-fiving each other with glee.

We commenced our descent down a series of switchbacks facing south towards the folds of the Zanskar Range and the snow-capped summits of the main Himalaya Range. On the other side of the pass, we were astounded to see Lobzang produce a 'hot' lunch for all of us. He had carried 20 kilograms of hot food all that way. It was another incredible feat on his part. As we sat down in the sunshine, out came rice, pita bread and hot dishes of red kidney beans, eggplant and curried vegetables. It was a huge surprise and truly wonderful.

We walked 'down' for the rest of the day, gradually descending for a further 2625 feet, to a point where the trail petered out. Lobzang had gone on ahead to coordinate the cleaning of our wet, muddy tents from the night before. We waited for Raj and the snails of the group to catch up and continued to our camp near the village of Shingo at 13,615 feet. After an eight-hour walk, yoga was just what we needed to end the day.

The World is Your Pearl

**Another vertigo moment
Photos – Niall MacNeill**

Trekking Ladakh—An Epic Journey ~ 2015 ~

My journal notes described the next day's events, which turned out to be an adventure of epic proportions, and far different from our trip notes, which read:

> ~ *"Below Shogdo, the trail enters a narrow gorge where willow, poplar and Himalayan musk rose provide a natural canopy alongside the river course. The Skiu Monastery (at 11,270 feet) marks the confluence of the stream coming from Shogdo and the Markha Valley. From Skiu we head down to the rope bridge over the Zanskar River before reaching the village of Chilling where we will transfer by road to Alchi."* ~

However, this day turned out to be 'hellish'. Yoga this morning was lovely in the sunshine before we commenced the walk from camp with clear blue skies. Breathing was easy as we descended through a very pretty valley with pack horses and donkeys passing us all the while.

At one point the horses carrying our red bags started to bolt fast, and took off down the narrow trail with the rocky river far below. Lobzang was ahead of them. He turned to stand in the middle of the trail, and held up his hands to stop them as they rushed towards him. They began slowing as Lobzang spoke to them. His calm face was truly Zen. They were really hedging to move, bucking and straining. He soothed them and made them all wait, then said something to them, releasing them one at a time to amble slowly down the mountainside. To me it was a heart-stopping moment, but he was unfazed and in complete control.

This morning's walk from camp to lunch included eighteen river crossings where Lobzang and the boys placed huge rocks at various points in the fast-moving river for us to cross. At one point Lobzang offered to carry us across "with our packs on". This was where we just gave up on preserving our walking boots and stepped in to wade across through the fast-running water.

The World is Your Pearl

The grandeur of each landscape we saw was hard to put into words. It was *so* remote, awe-inspiring, vast and desolate. The sheer power of the soaring walls of rock made us look like ants within a monolith.

At the bottom, we arrived in the little village of Skiu, and were invited to sit in the shade under the canopy of an abandoned parachute with an ancient old blacksmith who was blind in one eye. He forged something in iron while fanning his coals with a bellows made from sheepskin.

Once again, small lunches, packed in plastic bags, were produced from the bag which Lobzang had carried all the way over so many river crossings since leaving camp this morning.

Julie was feeling ill with some kind of stomach problem and was in such a bad way she couldn't go on. She was taken to one of the little village houses where she slept solidly on the floor for two hours while Lobzang and Campbell left to go ahead to try to get transport. The rest of us set out walking with Raj on the next leg of our journey through the valley.

It was hot, and I was glad I'd borrowed an umbrella from the hotel back in Leh. Mary and a couple of others stayed back with Julie while we walked to the Zanskar River, visible from a vast distance above. At times we became separated, and strung out as we walked at different paces. On a couple of occasions I found myself alone and frozen on the spot with phobia from the height, having to wait for someone to catch up to release me once again from my stricken state.

Our circumstances became bizarre. We were required to drink as much as possible at altitude, and especially in the heat of the day, so the reality of this in this barren landscape with no foliage to hide behind was that I came to the point where trying to become separated was the only way I could just sit down to have a pee. Occasionally I could get ahead and go behind a boulder and hope nobody came from the other direction. At one point I thought to go around the bend of a trail which went off the main road, as two of the girls, both named Belinda, stood guard for me on the hairpin bend of the road.

That turned out to be a very bad move, as the trail petered out on a steep precipice. Belinda happened to look across and said, "Are you all right?" I was stricken again, hanging by my fingernails in terror of my feet slipping backwards on the shale stones. This would have been a slip of four or five hundred feet. She came across and took my hand. This released my brain and I could walk back out to where I just sat down on the road and 'went' minutes before the truck came along with everyone in it. We climbed aboard. Seventeen of us stood up on the back of a small tray truck as it swerved around steep hairpin bends along the crumbling, stony roads. It was a terrifying experience as we screamed with nervous

The World is Your Pearl

The Indus Valley

laughter, clinging on to each other and hanging on for grim death all the way to the bottom.

We heaved a sigh of relief as we staggered off the back of the truck with shaking knees, only to discover that the rope bridge which should have been there for us to cross the Indus River had been washed away two months before by torrential flooding which had swept through the valley. Instead of walking across, we were crammed into box trolleys, three people to a basket, and pulled 350 feet across from the other side by men hauling rope pulleys linked to a cable 20 feet above the swirling, icy water.

This was the point where we were to be met by our vehicles and transported a further 43 kilometres to our hotel for hot showers and a meal after the trek.

Box trolley crossing the Indus

Instead, the adventure continued. We had to keep walking, as five landslides had destroyed the road during the storms we'd experienced on our trek. Having left camp that morning at 8:00 a.m., we'd already walked for 11 kilometres over steep and rough terrain and were becoming foot sore.

The skies turned black as another thunderstorm was brewing. None of us took any photographs as it was too dangerous for any of us to do anything but concentrate on where we placed our feet between the rocks and rubble. The massive overhangs were ominous above as the thunder clapped and the rains came. The landslides had fallen across the road we had taken from Chilling to do our white water rafting before the trek. As we passed the point where our rafting had commenced only days before, I knew we had at least a further 20 kilometres to walk.

The World is Your Pearl

Loose rocks continued to fall and the rain really started pouring as the day was closing in and it was getting dark. I knew how unsafe the road was because we had travelled beneath it on the raft, and tried not to think of those little marker rocks which indicated where the road was crumbling and where cars and trucks should *not* drive. In a few minutes it would be pitch dark with no way of seeing where I was walking.

Boulders the size of a three-storey house hung overhead above the scree slopes.

The rain was pouring, and I had a plastic poncho covering my pack. I carried my closed umbrella as it would have blown inside-out in the wind. Out there, in all this craziness of nature, I was as worried about my iPad and iPhone getting wet as I was about my life. I couldn't do much about either.

All of us had split up. Just doing what we could to keep going. All the while, I was looking up at the ominous loose rocks above. Many were monstrous in size, and looked as though they were just balancing on the edge. Luckily the thunder wasn't rocking the earth as it had two nights ago.

Things were getting grim, and for some reason I was suddenly in agony with a pain in my right foot, which caused me to start limping.

The body endured a lot in various ways at altitude, and it was imperative to drink water constantly to avoid dehydration which resulted in thumping headaches. I tried to keep drinking but needed to pee again. The rain was coming down so hard I didn't even care. It was too wet to go for the packet of tissues I had in my pocket.

Just as darkness really fell, I saw the lights of vehicles ahead. We'd walked and limped for 20 kilometres (equivalent, I was told, to 30 kilometres due to the extremes in height). The army had been brought in to clear the landslides to this point so we were rescued in a big rusty truck. It was like a container on wheels, with no windows, and a canvas over the top. We threw everything in and were lifted up in saturated heaps to sit against the rusty walls where we bumped along the dangerous road above the river.

We hadn't gone far when we stopped again. Our red bags had somehow been brought to this point and were laying in the mud on the side of the road. These were loaded in and walled up around us in the truck. We were eventually transported across the cleared, but rubbly remains of the landslides to awaiting 4WD vehicles which took us a further one-and-a-half-hour drive to our homestay in Alchi.

This was reported to be one of the better homestays in the area. As we limped along with our leg muscles now seizing up, we were ushered in the dark along a concrete pathway with deep open drains. At one point there was a two-foot-square hole in the middle of the path, only visible to the front person holding a mobile phone torchlight.

Once inside our homestay with our bags, I climbed the stairs to my allocated room, stripped off my wet, muddy clothes, only to find ice-cold water through all the taps. I washed the mud off, dressed, and went downstairs to discover that our sad and sorry group of Aussies had to opt for a 'Dingo's Dinner' ... *a drink of water and a look around!*

The staff were expecting us to arrive between 4:00 and 6:00 p.m. when the hot water was ready for our showers, and our hot meals had been prepared. By the time 9:30 came, they'd given up, thinking we weren't coming. The staff rustled up a hot cup of tea for us and I fell into bed and died for the night.

The contrast of our remote experience when we arrived back in Leh was the realisation that progress was changing the face of this harmonious society.

The World is Your Pearl

The creeping-in of Westernisation meant that people were having to buy the things they were once able to produce. Their communities were being fragmented. The men were not on their own land to do their share of the work. Life was speeding up rapidly and there was no longer the time to live life as they once did. Herbicides and insecticides, now banned in Western society, were being used in these once pristine organic valleys. Their air was being choked with fumes from vehicles and machinery where animals had once been their only means of labour.

I purchased a wonderful book called *Ancient Futures* written by Helena Norberg-Hodge. It described the lives and systems of these beautiful people whose philosophies and lifestyles we would all benefit from returning to. They were living proof of the sort of abundant and harmonious life which could be achieved even in such harsh conditions at altitude in extremes of temperatures at the most basic level of existence with almost nothing but hand-held tools and human resilience, and where kindness abounded.

~ Epilogue ~

This has been a dip into the ocean of my many travels to over 40 countries.

At the time of writing, I had just returned from Mexico and Cuba where our cycling adventure was cut short by the worldwide pandemic of the COVID-19 coronavirus in March 2020.

Once again, I was blessed with good fortune in three ways. Five days before my return, my daughter Emma was required to have a caesarean for the birth of my second grandchild, Willow. The Box Hill Hospital was only just beginning to deal with virus patients. Emma and Willow were released a day before things escalated to more major proportions.

My trip was magnificent to the final moment as life folded in behind and around us on our return to Australian soil. We flew without drama or delays from Havana, Cuba, to Cancun, Mexico, to Los Angeles, USA immigration, where, on our way *to* Mexico less than a month ago, we'd queued along with 3000 people for two and a half hours on a normal day.

Now, LA immigration was empty but for us and a few stragglers as we journeyed back to Melbourne, where we were directed straight into isolation inside our homes for two weeks. Three days after returning to my home, other travellers filtering back into Australia were forced to isolate in hotel rooms rather than return to their houses.

Ours would be the last run for our airline crew as flights worldwide began to shut down. Borders closed, cruise ships were stranded, unable to dock, countries cut themselves off, and businesses (except for essential services) closed down. Schools, pubs, clubs, sports events, theatres and churches closed. Weddings halted, funeral attendees were limited and schooling was to be conducted remotely.

People were trapped in other countries unable to return home and required to self-isolate in overseas hotel rooms for untold weeks. Airlines collapsed, many thousands of jobs were lost and the worldwide economy plummeted.

Life as we knew it was forced to slow down almost to a stop. As whole families had to stay home to isolate against the spreading virus, uncertainty abounded. By September 2020, there had been 33 million infections causing 1,000,000 to die worldwide. The numbers continued to rise as medical scientists raced to find a vaccine.

Through all of this, however, because the earth's inhabitants were required to slow their pace and learn to be happy to live with less, strange but wonderful things also began to occur. Air, sea and land travel were required to grind almost to a halt. NASA's photographs from outer space showed that air pollution was clearing all over the world presenting many positive indicators, including the Himalayas, now visible from India for the first time in decades.

In all of this, one thing was certain: Mother Nature will always prevail, and our beautiful earth will soon be slightly cleaner, and a more wondrous place to explore.

~ Glenda's Tips and Tricks for Adventure Travel ~

~ Don't be so cautious that you forget to live ~

1. Don't just wish you could travel and explore, *commit* and make it happen.

    Desire is the greatest motivator there is. When you have a destination in mind, book the trip a year ahead, pay the deposit then find the money to pay it off in manageable instalments leading up to it. As the saying goes, Just Do It!

    As a teenager, planning my first interstate holiday, I saved by taking on babysitting at nights in addition to my day job.

    Where there's a will there's a way, but remember that once the travel bug bites, there's no known antidote. You'll want to experience adventures again and again.

2. Don't go just to look at a room. The money you save on fancy hotel rooms can be spent on 'experiences'. For me, accommodation is just a place to put my head and prepare to move on.

The World is Your Pearl

The best experiences are at ground level. By immersing in the lifestyles of the people, you get a feel for their lives by living with them. These can take the form of accommodations like riads or home-stays with the Berber tribes of Morocco, Gers and Yurts in Mongolia, tents or tea houses in Nepal, or tribal desert camps in Africa.

3. Don't drink the water. Bottled, sterilised or boiled water will ensure your trip is not delayed by gastro or dysentery, or worse.

4. Be open. Travel adventure is about possibility and discovery. Stay loose and experience the delights of the world without judgement or expectation.

5. Consider the customs of the people; be curious but go lightly with respect, and interact with them.

6. Challenge packing light. The less you can take, the less encumbered you'll be. Carrying too much stuff is a burden.

   There are many packing lists to source online.

7. Active human-powered adventure is a sustainable way to experience the essence of a destination. As you immerse yourself in a place, it will become a part of you. By riding, trekking or just walking through it, you interact with nature, the land and its people.

8. Don't take unreasonable risks. Remember that your actions will impact on the entire expedition, so work reasonably as a team.

9. Read a book about the place you're visiting to learn more about the people, their customs and way of life.

~ Glenda's Tips and Tricks for Adventure Travel ~

10. Go somewhere off the beaten track. The best way for an adventurist to see the world safely is when all the hard work has been taken out of it by the right adventure company. They will plan out the route, provide crews, provisions and all the equipment. This takes the expense and hardship away and ensures a great experience.

11. Guard your passport and money with your life.

    These are your lifeline and it's best to guard them as though there's a pickpocket around every corner. It's sad to say this, as 95% of humanity are honest and decent, but on the chance that you encounter one of the remaining 5% it's best to err on the side of caution at all times to avoid extreme inconvenience and disruption to your travels.

12. Travel insurance is a 'must' for all overseas trips, without exception. In most cases it is a prerequisite for adventure travel.

13. In the event of an accident, or lost or stolen items, always get a police report. You won't be able to claim through insurance without one.

14. Ensure your passport has a minimum six months validity.

15. Keep your passport in good condition. Water damaged or folded pages causing destruction of passport information will result in you being turned away at the boarding gate and forfeiting your travel.

16. Scan your passport, flight tickets, travel insurance, visas, wilderness passes and travel documents, and email them to yourself so you can access them on the worldwide web if they are lost. Another friend saves them to a USB which he wears around his neck from the time he leaves home. Otherwise take

photos of everything and store them on your phone—or do all three.

17. A great option for travelling light is to have a well-planned clothing system. Layers of garments including polar fleece, thermals, fine merino, lightweight, drip-dry and wicking fabrics, are quite expensive, but well worth the money and will last a lifetime with the right care.

18. The best favour you can do yourself is to purchase the most expensive walking boots you can afford, as well as good woollen trekking socks. These are your ticket to freedom. If your feet are comfortable in good footwear, you won't have a problem. I've seen people in agony with joint pain and weeping blisters, wearing runners which didn't give the right ankle support or sole grip.

    Be sure to wear the boots in for a good six months before your trek.

19. On steep treks such as the Overland Track in Tasmania, or the mountains of Nepal, a trekking pole really helps to support and stabilise knees and ankles, particularly when carrying a heavy pack on the steep downhills.

20. I never go anywhere without a small umbrella. Even with a rain jacket and wet weather gear, I feel so much better in a downpour if my head and shoulders stay dry. The same goes for blasting sun. Even though I'm a major sun goddess, there are times on a trek when the sun is so searing, an umbrella is a wonderful shield against the burning heat.

21. To keep the weight of a pack down, Chux wipes can be used in place of a towel and can be rinsed out and dried by pegging to the pack.

~ Glenda's Tips and Tricks for Adventure Travel ~

22. Snacks and provisions: Although I don't eat lollies at home, I always take a stash of things like toffee, caramel, nut bars, almonds, coffee bags and tea bags on every trip. The fresh air and exercise gives me an appetite for something sweet and these sustain me along the way when I'm feeling peckish. It's a treat to have a really good coffee, or an English breakfast tea when the kettle boils somewhere in a remote place.

23. A small first aid kit, including antiseptic, blister blocks, gastro stop, electrolyte sachets, cold and flu caps, Band-Aids/plasters, sting spray, insect repellent and painkillers are essential in your packing kit.

24. I take about 200 AUD worth of local currency to tide me over when I arrive in any country, then use my credit card for everything else. I can withdraw money as needed from ATMs when inside civilisation, anywhere in the world. Gone are the days of travellers cheques or carrying loads of cash. Not a lot of money is required while trekking or cycling as most meals are provided on the trip. You may require cash for alcohol, or to purchase a local handcraft or to pay an entry fee for an optional side experience along the way.

25. Have money set aside as tips for crew and porters so you know you've got it for them at the end.

26. Although clean mattresses, down jackets and sleeping bags are provided by World Expeditions, another luxury I sometimes take along with me on a trek is a small inflatable down mat for an extra layer of comfort.

27. A pillowcase-size drawstring bag is useful to stow clothes and doubles as a pillow.

28. I take a laundry kit. A travel clothesline with hooks at each end. A few little pegs. A couple of small plastic coat hangers. Two sizes of sink plugs for remote laundry troughs, and a small bottle of laundry concentrate or block of laundry soap. Hotel shampoos are also useful for washing clothes and smell nice.

29. Wring out wet smalls by laying on a towel. Roll up and twist to remove surplus water. Stow in a shower cap inside luggage, then hang it out at the next stop.

30. Stuffer bags are excellent for keeping all your gear separate and staying organised inside your luggage. They are lightweight nylon mesh packing bags with zipper closings and can be purchased online.

31. Check and double check that all required travel documents have been arranged and applied for well ahead of time. Visas, permits, wilderness passes, ESTAs (Electronic System for US Travel Authorisation) if travelling to, or passing through, America.

32. Check which vaccines and malaria precautions are required ahead of travel.

33. A small head torch helps in the middle of the night to allow hands free while rummaging around in the tent or having to venture out.

34. A cheap raffia bag is handy to stow in the bottom of your luggage in case you have to go off on a side trip overnight and don't want to take all your gear, or if you're a shopper and tend to bring back more than you took away.

35. To ensure you're not disappointed by missing out on activities you're keen to experience in any destination, it's wise to book online ahead of the trip.

~ Glenda's Tips and Tricks for Adventure Travel ~

36. Print out all receipts and vouchers for any pre-purchased activities and take them as hard copy proof of payment in your travel wallet.

37. When deciding to trek at altitude, ensure you start at the lowest point and work your way up to where the air is thinner in order to acclimatise.

38. Don't be tempted to start taking altitude sickness tablets too soon, as this can mask the symptoms. Always take advice from trained guides as to the appropriate timing.

39. If you're a seasoned traveller, create a 'Packing Bible'. I've written all my packing lists into a small exercise book. It includes:

    Packing for treks
    Packing for cycling trips
    Packing for tropical places
    Packing for a single-day hike
    Packing for picnics

    I mark it with ticks with a pencil as I'm packing, then rub out the ticks, ready for the next trip.

40. Where aircraft luggage weight is an issue, stow heaviest items in your carry-on bag.

41. Check Australian quarantine regulations before purchasing items overseas, such as wood, shells, nuts, skins, artefacts, foodstuff, etc.

42. If trekking through rural areas overseas, scrub your trekking boots with soapy water to ensure no disease from farm animals is brought back into Australia. I carry them back in my hand luggage for ease of inspection by the quarantine officers in

The World is Your Pearl

Customs. This saves a heap of time if they have to take them away to clean them.

43. Declare everything, and have items ready to show when you land, either in your hand luggage or where they can easily be found in your checked baggage. This can avoid a full unpack by officials, and affords a speedy exit from the airport.

44. The more training you can do to prepare your fitness and skills before the trip, the better experience you will have.

CELEBRATING
ADVENTURE

Here at World Expeditions, we thrive on helping people achieve their goal of experiencing the world authentically. We are thankful to Glenda for choosing us as her preferred tour company for so long and privileged to have shared her remarkable journey to so many interesting and out-of-the-way places over many decades.

Like many of our clients, Glenda embraces adventure, seeing it as a way to continually grow and learn more about herself and this amazing world in which we live. Combined with her innate curiosity, this adventurous spirit makes Glenda the ideal World Expeditions traveller.

Since Glenda's first trip with us, we've continually strived to go the extra mile, building our reputation on our pioneering style, with new ways of travelling and new destinations.

Thank you Glenda

— on the trail of adventure since 1975 —

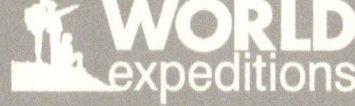

big adventures • small footprint | worldexpeditions.com

~ About the Author ~

Glenda is an author, artist and illustrator with a love of extreme adventure travel. She has visited more than 40 countries and lives an idyllic life between family, art and travel. As an art show judge and a private tutor of oil painting, watercolour, drawing and glass mosaic, she has taught in galleries and her home studio since 1989. Once a member of the Victorian Artists Society and an executive of the Sherbrooke Artists Society in Victoria, she organised landscape painting expeditions and workshops for groups of artists. Through her joy of writing and book illustration, she has produced four colourful children's books and two books of inspirational quotes and sayings. Her studio is a mecca for creative people, with drawing and painting classes for adults and children.

She was invited to have her work published in the book *Fifty Australian Artists* produced by Artists Ink, in aid of the Fred Hollows Foundation. Glenda has written **The World Is Your Pearl** to share just a few of her stories of adventure travel, and is available for speaker events.

Her books, art and contact details can be discovered on her website:

www.glendawisebooks.com

~ Acknowledgements ~

I would like to thank The Ultimate 48 Hour Author team and everyone who assisted me on my journey in the production of this book.

Emma Wise; Sam Benton; Mary Moody; Allison Perry; Kim Peterson; Elizabeth Halanga Kahia; Arthur Perry; Annie Watkins; Jon Bate; Peter Warren; Dennis Dawson; Mike Litchfield; Phil Jones; Margaret Bennett; Pam Freeman; Karen & David Brown; Christine Green; Mike Buxton; Scott Pinnegar; Peter Wise; Andrew Hart; Andrew Dunne; Vivienne Sanders and Linton Harris; Claire and Stephen Bridgeman; Niall MacNeill; Julie Jarvis; Joan Kimberley; Debra Hunter; Judy Wolff.

Speaker Bio >

GLENDA WISE

THE WORLD IS YOUR PEARL

'There is a way that Glenda embraces the world that is both refreshing and addictive'
~ Mary Moody ~

is an artist, illustrator and author, with a big passion for adventure. She has written and published her new book, The World is your Pearl, where she shares a few of her extreme adventures.

Outside the scope of high-end travel staying in luxury hotels and resorts, the true essence of a remote experience for Glenda requires sleeping in tents, tea houses, trucks, boats, yurts, riads, caves or tribal homes, and once under the wing of her brother's aeroplane. She has had many epic experiences through safe travel on a comparative shoestring with the right support.

After divorce from the man who remains one of her best friends, her two children having grown and left home, and the loss of her only brother in a tragic workplace accident, Glenda embarks on a completely new journey. She shares an inspiring account of how she got out into the world of adventure after loss and sadness.

Inspired by earlier experiences with her brother in the wilds of Bougainville, Glenda shifted her mind-set and now travels off the beaten track and often way out of her comfort zone. She describes some of her many amazing trips, trekking, cycling and exploring (often at altitude), visiting cultures which are remote and ancient in their customs and lifestyles.

In her exciting and engaging talks, Glenda describes:
. How to sneak up on adventure
. How to go about achieving it
. How to get started the very first time
. How to conquer your fears
. How to keep having adventures at any age
. What you'll tell your grandchildren

To enquire about engaging Glenda as a speaker at your next event, contact her below for availabilities and pricing. Glenda can adapt her talks to suit your event's timing and audience.

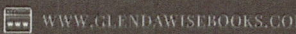
WWW.GLENDAWISEBOOKS.COM

PEARLYTRAVELLER@GMAIL.COM

~ Notes ~

The World is Your Pearl

~ Notes ~

www.ingramcontent.com/pod-product-compliance
Lightning Source LLC
Chambersburg PA
CBHW021431080526
44588CB00009B/492